Leading Up

Transformational Leadership for Fundraisers

Leading Up

Transformational
Leadership
for Fundraisers

LILYA WAGNER

WILEY

John Wiley & Sons, Inc.

Library of Congress Cataloging-in-Publication Data
Wagner, Lilya.
  Leading up : transformational leadership for fundraisers / Lilya Wagner.
    p.   cm. — (The AFP fund development series)
  Includes bibliographical references and index.
  ISBN-10: 0-471-69718-4 (cloth)
  ISBN-13: 978-0-471-69718-3 (cloth)
    1. Fund raising. 2. Leadership. I. Title. II. Series
HV41.2.W34   2005
658.15'224— dc22

                                                            2005050355

Printed in the United States of America

10 9 8 7 6 5 4 3 2 1

This book is dedicated to my colleagues and friends of The Fund Raising School, with whom I worked from 1991–2005—to all staff, directors Bob Fogal and Tim Seiler, and faculty. Thank you for supporting my efforts and work, for providing opportunities for me to excel, and for the pleasure of working with you.

The AFP Fund Development Series

The AFP Fund Development Series is intended to provide fund development professionals and volunteers, including board members (and others interested in the nonprofit sector), with top-quality publications that help advance philanthropy as voluntary action for the public good. Our goal is to provide practical, timely guidance and information on fundraising, charitable giving, and related subjects. The Association of Fundraising Professionals (AFP) and Wiley each bring to this innovative collaboration unique and important resources that result in a whole greater than the sum of its parts. For information on other books in the series, please visit:

http://www.afpnet.org

THE ASSOCIATION OF FUNDRAISING PROFESSIONALS

The Association of Fundraising Professionals (AFP) represents 26,000 members in more than 170 chapters throughout the world, working to advance philanthropy through advocacy, research, education, and certification programs. The association fosters development and growth of fundraising professionals and promotes high ethical standards in the fundraising profession. For more information or to join the world's largest association of fundraising professionals, visit *www.afpnet.org*.

2005-2006 AFP Publishing Advisory Committee

Linda L. Chew, CFRE, Chair
Associate Director, Alta Bates Summit Foundation

Nina P. Berkheiser, CFRE
Director of Development, SPCA Tampa Bay

D. C. Dreger, ACFRE
Senior Campaign Director, Custom Development Solutions (CDS)

Samuel N. Gough, CFRE
Principal, The AFRAM Group

Audrey P. Kintzi, ACFRE
Chief Advancement Officer, Girl Scout Council St. Croix Valley

Robert Mueller, CFRE
Vice President, Hospice Foundation of Louisville

Maria Elena Noriega
Director, Noriega Malo & Associates

Leslie E. Weir, MA, ACFRE
Director of Gift Planning, Health Sciences Centre Foundation

Sharon R. Will, CFRE
Director of Development, South Wind Hospice

John Wiley & Sons
Susan McDermott
Senior Editor (Professional/Trade Division), John Wiley & Sons

AFP Staff
Jan Alfieri
Manager, New Product Development

Walter Sczudlo
Executive Vice President & General Counsel

Contents

Preface

Fundraising professionals must employ many leadership skills in order to carry out their responsibilities, yet many are not in top or designated leadership positions. As a result, if they are successful, they provide leadership in the truest sense—leadership that doesn't come from position or power but leadership that is built on proven characteristics. Leaders in fundraising motivate, serve as examples, manage, communicate, and make renewal possible. Leading without authority isn't easy, but is essential for the successful fundraising professional. The plethora of books that are available on leadership—books that have a variety of approaches and viewpoints—provide little discussion on leading up. Even though the topic has increased in coverage and popularity, there are very few materials that apply leadership principles and practices specifically to the fundraising profession and professional. Fundraisers deserve to know and be taught how to assess their own personal working situations and consider responsibility without authority. Through this book, they can determine what leadership strategies can be used to reach fundraising goals that benefit the organization and its mission, as well as enhance their personal achievement records, while adhering to their own missions and goals.

Acknowledgments

With much appreciation to Timothy L. Seiler, director, The Fund Raising School at the Center on Philanthropy (Indiana University), and to Lelei LeLaulu, President and CEO, Counterpart International, Washington, DC, for reviewing this manuscript and suggesting changes that improved the content.

About the Author

Lilya Wagner, EdD, CFRE, is Vice-President for Philanthropy at Counterpart International, based in Washington, DC. Previously, she served at the Center on Philanthropy and The Fund Raising School at Indiana University, where she was also director of the Women's Philanthropy Institute.

Introduction

Life is like a jigsaw puzzle but you don't have the picture on the front of the box to know what it's supposed to look like. Sometimes, you're not even sure if you have all of the pieces."[1] This comment is taken from *A Whack on the Side of the Head* by Roger Von Oech. Von Oech believes that there are two main phases in the development of new ideas: an imaginative phase and a practical one. The motto of the first phase is "thinking something different," and the motto of the second phase is "getting something done."[2]

Fundraising professionals are required to engage in both phases—they must accomplish goals and meet expectations, and yet they must also be creative in managing their programs because of the dynamic state of the profession. The concept of leadership in fundraising takes on both phases described by von Oech—fundraising professionals have to get things done but they also need to exercise leadership from whatever rank or position they hold in order to motivate others, and this

---

[1] Roger Von Oech, *A Whack on the Side of the Head,* 3rd edition (New York: Warner Books, 1998), p. 53.

[2] *Ibid.,* p. 42.

1

means "thinking something different." That's what this book is about. The essential questions it raises are:

- How do I get things done when I'm not in charge?
- How do I motivate others when I don't have formal authority?
- How do I convince or persuade my colleagues and superiors of the need for their action and involvement?
- How can I lead when I'm not a recognized leader by virtue of power or position?

The premise is that everyone in the fundraising profession can be and must be a leader and must exercise leadership traits and develop leadership qualities no matter his or her job or position. A leader is one who breaks new paths into unfamiliar territory, recognizes a problem before it turns into an emergency, is reasonable and calm, submerges himself or herself[3] in the fountain of the people, implements noble ideas, is practical and a realist, is a visionary and an idealist, and, sometimes, is the wave pushed ahead by the ship![4] Many of the traditional qualities of leadership, as will be discussed in this book, apply not just to those who are in recognizable, appointed, usurped, or elected positions of power but also to those who are outside the realm of formal authority. Leadership qualities have to be learned and practiced by all who wish to achieve in fundraising, whether they are the boss or not.

The words of James Kilpatrick are particularly appealing: "Find out where the people want to go, then hustle yourself around in front of

---

[3] In order to avoid cumbersome language use, I will alternate the use of gender, sometimes referring to the feminine and sometimes to the masculine, since leadership is gender neutral.

[4] Paraphrased from "Leader," *Dictionary of Quotable Definitions* by Eugene E. Brussell (Englewood Cliffs, NJ: Prentice-Hall, 1970), pp. 323–324. The last phrase is by Leo Tolstoy.

them."[5] This implies that we must listen, analyze, and influence, whether or not our position is one of power. Fundraising professionals have learned that in order to be successful in our demanding profession, we have to learn the art of leading up, which is equivalent to the practice "lateral leadership,"[6] a phrase coined by Harvard negotiation specialist Roger Fisher and his colleague Alan Sharp. As described in an issue of *Harvard Management Update,* a leader is defined by a set of attributes, attitudes, and habits that set a person apart from others. Real leadership has never been about authority, positions of power, or dogmatic dictatorship. It's about listening, valuing, following advice, and bringing people together for a common goal and vision.

Fundraising professionals often practice leadership without even consciously realizing it. They serve by example, motivate others to action, exercise influence, develop and share a vision, help others catch the vision, plan and lead the action, consider the desires and feelings of others, achieve consensus in a group, and obtain practical results. The leadership skills that fundraisers use range from the concrete, such as bringing a group together for planning, to the ephemeral, such as developing and sharing a vision of what can be.

Fundraising is a noble profession that takes a person beyond mere technique to a higher plane of thought and action. The ideal professional is one who thinks about what he does, implements principles instead of following technical blueprints, and has an ethical basis for what he does.

This book takes up where many others leave off. Leadership books number in the thousands. Many excellent volumes are quoted and

---

[5] As quoted in *Good Advice* by William Safire and Leonard Safir (New York: Wing Books, 1982), p. 195.

[6] *Harvard Management Update* (March 2000) presents this concept by Harvard negotiation specialist Roger Fisher and colleague Alan Sharp.

referred to, and many others are listed in the appendices and readings lists. Leadership books that discuss leading from the middle are fewer. While recognition of leadership as a quality that doesn't stem from authority of power has been a recurring theme, an application of such leadership to fundraising has seldom occurred. Therefore, this book has a unique purpose. It makes a case for leading up and expresses that case in principle and in practice so that others can not only build up their causes and organizations but also can influence a professional field that is still developing.

Lessons on Leadership from Lincoln

- *Build strong, interpersonal relationships and bonds.*
- *Invest time and money in better understanding the ins and outs of human nature.*
- *Show your compassionate and caring nature.*
- *When you extinguish hope, you create desperation.*
- *Be poised and confident under pressure.*
- *A dictatorial type of leadership doesn't work. Coercion and force negate the rights of the individual.*
- *Be smart enough to know you can't do it all.*
- *Any successful organization, whether a business or a country, must possess strong shared values. These values must be owned by the members.*
- *It is your duty to advance the aims of the organization and also to help those who serve it.*
- *Pettiness, spite, and vengeance are beneath the dignity of a leader.*
- *Ignore most critical attacks, but fight back when they are important enough to make a difference.*
- *Maintain grace under pressure.*
- *Listen to people and be guided by them.*

(continues)

- *There will be failures. Persevere and learn from these failures.*
- *Be inquisitive and willing to learn.*
- *Be careful about what you say and think before you speak.*
- *Preach a vision and continually reaffirm it.*

—Donald T. Phillips[7]

Part One of this book, "Breaking Old Molds, Accepting New Concepts of Leadership," presents a knowledge base on leadership and surveys accepted concepts and tactics that guide the thinking and practice of leadership. These lay the groundwork for considering traits and characteristics that are desirable for successfully leading up in the fundraising profession. Leading in the real world necessitates a reality check on fundraisers' roles and how they get things done when they are not in charge. The need for and ability to change will result in a consideration of what attitudes and actions must be modified as leadership roles in fundraising are adopted.

Part Two, "Leadership Traits and Characteristics and Their Applicability to Fundraising," considers the challenges that fundraisers encounter when working with people and processes that move the organization toward its primary mission. It considers a "they" and "us" situation, and addresses the differences between those who have designated power and identified leadership status and those of us who will lead up. To help accomplish this, a new model for leading up is presented, bolstered by adaptations of applicable concepts such as those of Robert K. Greenleaf—concepts that are highly adaptable for fundraisers and the roles they play. This section addresses the most salient

---

[7] Adapted from Phillips, *Lincoln on Leadership: Executive Strategies for Tough Times* (New York: Warner Books, 1992).

concepts that fundraisers must have to become leaders—not by position or power but by exercising those characteristics that define true leadership. The concepts include:

- Leading for loyalty
- Leading for innovation
- Leading to build
- Balancing humility and assertiveness
- Facilitative leadership
- Emotional intelligence
- Ethical practice
- Diversity and multicultural challenges
- Leading from mission
- Survival versus vision

Part Three, "Transforming Yourself: Meeting the Challenge of Leading Up," helps you transform yourself and build your capability for meeting the challenges of leading from the middle. Specific steps are outlined that help you become an effective leader in your position.

Any leadership skill at any level requires thinking in new, creative, innovative, and different ways. For example, in the winter of 333 B.C., Alexander the Great arrives in Asia and settles down for the winter in the city of Gordium. Alexander hears the legend of the Gordian knot—anyone who can untie this odd and complicated knot will be king of Asia. Alexander asks to see the knot and studies it for a bit. Certainly, it is complicated and has him baffled. After some reflection and frustration, a bright idea dawns. He whips out his sword and slices the knot in half. Asia is his.

Good fundraisers follow good rules, but sometimes they have to look beyond the expected and challenge the rules. They have to cycle

> *Leadership is giving. Leadership is an ethic, a gift of oneself. It is easy to miss the depth and power of this message. . . . The essence of leadership is not giving things or even providing visions. It is offering oneself and one's spirit. . . . Your quest as a leader is "a journey to find the treasure of your true self, then to return home to give your gift to help transform the kingdom—and in the process, your own life."*
>
> —Lee G. Bolman and Terrance E. Deal[8]

out obsolete ideas and cycle in new ones that help them look at traditional concepts and principles in new ways. That's the way it is with leadership. As von Oech said, "Life is like a banana. You start out green and get soft and mushy with age. Some people want to be one of the bunch while others want to be top banana. You have to take care not to slip on the externals. And, finally, you have to strip off the outer coating to get at the meat."[9] I hope you will find plenty of "meat" in this book that will help you practice the effective principles of leadership, of "leading up" in your fundraising career. Victor Hugo said, "There is one thing more powerful than all the armies of the world; and that is an idea whose time has come."[10] The time has come for all fundraisers to be leaders, for the benefit of the donor, the constituents, the organization, and themselves.

---

[8] Lee G. Bolman and Terrance E. Deal, *Leading with Soul: An Uncommon Journey of Spirit* (San Francisco: Jossey-Bass, 2001).

[9] Von Oech, p. 52.

[10] Quoted in Karl Albrecht, *The Northbound Train* (New York: AMACOM, 1994), p. 164.

REFLECTIONS

Mind mapping is a great way to explore an idea or come up with fresh thinking.

Take a piece of paper, preferably from a flip chart, although any blank piece will do. In the center, write your name and three characteristics or traits you believe describe yourself. Let your mind wander (something we can't often allow our minds to do while managing fundraising, so this is a luxury) and think about the following. Jot down ideas in creative ways. Don't try to answer these questions in order, or even answer them all. Let one question lead to another thought or question.

- When did you use your leadership traits to your advantage?
- When did you fail to use leadership traits and regretted it?
- Whom do you admire as a leader?
- What traits does he or she have that you want to emulate?
- If you were asked to tell a story of a successful fundraising experience, what would it be?
- What fundraising experience have you had that taught you a valuable lesson? What was the lesson, and how would you teach it to others?

After you have generated plenty of ideas, thoughts, associations, and personal suggestions, do something else for a while. Then come back and look at what you wrote. Can you answer these questions for yourself?

- Selecting from what you have written, what leadership traits do you believe best describe you?
- Analyzing what you have written, what pattern do you see emerging?

- Write down one goal you wish to achieve in considering yourself as a leader.

DEVELOP YOUR SKILLS

This is a Leadership Assessment Diagnostic tool. It will help you assess your leadership skills by indicating areas for further development.

Scale

1 = Strongly Disagree   2 = Disagree   3 = Partly Agree
4 = Agree   5 = Strongly Agree

_____ 1. I balance focusing on the future with an understanding of present conditions and events from the past.

_____ 2. I support others to achieve their objectives through regular one-on-ones.

_____ 3. I am able to maintain self-awareness in the context of external interference, challenges, or unexpected events.

_____ 4. I take time to get updated on current events.

_____ 5. In conversation, I provide undivided attention, show interest, and suspend judgment.

_____ 6. I demonstrate integrity even in the face of challenges and adversities.

_____ 7. I show respect when questioning the ideas and opinions of others.

_____ 8. I challenge others to capitalize on their unrealized potential without putting them down.

(continues)

(Continued)

1 = Strongly Disagree   2 = Disagree   3 = Partly Agree
4 = Agree   5 = Strongly Agree

_____   9. I attend events that improve my professionalism.

_____   10. I explore, identify, and define the nature, cause, and implications of problems.

_____   11. I demonstrate consistency between expressed beliefs, values, and actions.

_____   12. I assist others in taking responsibility, setting goals, and taking planned action to solve problems.

_____   13. I assess which role is most appropriate for the person or situation—strategist, coaching, or content expert—and adjust accordingly.

_____   14. I possess an understanding of the operations of my organization.

_____   15. I manage time in a way that balances personal and professional objectives.

_____   16. I focus on actual results of a process or plan.

_____   17. I am able to build relationships, ask questions, and support a variety of initiatives to influence across the organization.

_____   18. I demonstrate an understanding of living and leading by example.

_____   19. I am able to identify and develop skills and effective behavior in others.

_____   20. I possess technical competence to achieve relevant goals and objectives.

_____   21. I consistently and clearly communicate the desired results of a process or plan.

(continues)

1 = Strongly Disagree	2 = Disagree	3 = Partly Agree
4 = Agree	5 = Strongly Agree	

_____ 22. I align people's visions, values, goals, and action plans with those of the organization and the bigger picture.

_____ 23. I possess an understanding of professional trends.

_____ 24. I identify and facilitate to remedy self-defeating behaviors in myself and others.

_____ 25. I explore readiness to change and overcome the blocks to moving ahead by recognizing the stages of organizational development.

Interpretation of Leadership Skills Assessment

In the right-hand column put your score for the question indicated in the left. Then total your responses.

Question	Knowledge
4	
9	
14	
20	
23	
TOTAL	

Question	Strategy
1	
10	
16	
22	
25	
TOTAL	

Question	Communication
5	
7	
13	
17	
21	
TOTAL	

Question	Development
3	
8	
12	
19	
24	
TOTAL	

(continues)

(Continued)

Question	Self-Awareness
2	
6	
11	
15	
18	
TOTAL	

Now, add the totals in each section. Refer to the range of scores below to identify what type of further action you should take in each area of leadership.

1–10	You need to take immediate action to improve your skills, performance, and results. Consult a mentor and other resources available to you.
11–19	Develop action plans to be implemented in two weeks—this will get you on track for getting to the next level.
20–25	You are performing well as a leader. You may need specific action plans in pinpointed areas to optimize your performance.

Adapted from *Infoline, Leadership Development,* ASTD, January 2001. Used by permission.

FOR FURTHER READING

Additional readings can be found at the end of the book.

Bernard M. Bass. *Stogdill's Handbook of Leadership.* New York: The Free Press, a Division of Macmillan, 3rd Edition, 1990.

Geoffrey M. Bellman. *Getting Things Done When You Are Not in Charge: How to Succeed from a Support Position.* San Francisco: Berrett-Koehler, 1992.

Lee G. Bolman and Terrence E. Deal. *Leading with Soul: An Uncommon Journey of Spirit.* San Francisco: Jossey-Bass, 2001.

Gene Griessman. *The Words Lincoln Lived By.* New York: Fireside/ Simon & Schuster, 1997.

PART ONE

Breaking Old Molds, Accepting New Concepts of Leadership

CHAPTER 1

Defining Your Concept of Leadership

A look at personal perspectives and the knowledge base of leadership.

*C*ertain Trumpets is a book of stories about leaders—individuals who are well known to us because of the indelible mark they made on our historic paths. For each character portrayed, the author gives a characteristic that defines his or her leadership traits. For example:

- Electoral—Franklin Roosevelt
- Radical—Harriet Tubman
- Diplomatic—Andrew Young
- Military—Napoleon
- Constitutional—George Washington
- Intellectual—Socrates
- Rhetoric—Martin Luther King, Jr.
- Opportunistic—Cesare Borgia

The thoughtful stories told in *Certain Trumpets* portray the variety of leadership positions and qualities. Garry Willis, the author, says "We do not lack leaders. Various trumpets are always being sounded."[1]

Attempting to define leadership is much like attempting to define beauty; it's hard to explain, but you know it when you see it. The leader instills a passion and daring that gives subordinates the courage to act. But views of leadership can be motivating, inspiring, confusing, or daunting—or all of the above. Robert J. Lee and Sara N. King from the Center for Creative Leadership collected seven views or images of leadership they had identified. Each carries its own implications. Some are about who becomes a leader and how, while others are concerned with how a leader should lead. As you read, consider how these views may shape how you begin to think of yourself as a leader.

- **The Genetic View:** Some people are born with leadership talents; others are not. Therefore, leadership is an inborn talent.

- **The Learned View:** If you study leadership carefully and practice the principles, you too can be an effective leader. In other words, leadership can be learned.

- **The Heroic View:** Those who perform courageous, wise, and benevolent accomplishments are the best leaders—they get the rest of us out of trouble.

- **The Top-Only View:** Leadership happens only at or close to the top of an organization, and everyone else follows orders. If you're not the boss, you're nothing. If you're the boss, you're everything anyone would want to be.

- **The Social Script View:** When it's your time to be a leader, you'll be invited, and you should accept gratefully. After all, not everyone is asked.

---

[1] Garry Willis, *Certain Trumpets: The Call of Leaders* (New York: Simon & Schuster, 1994), p. 22.

- **The Position View:** If you have the right title for the right job, you're a leader. This is a traditionally bureaucratic view. If you're "president of . . ." your leadership virtue is assumed.

- **The Calling View:** While not necessarily a religious experience, a call to lead can be so powerful that you have little control over its inevitability. Others shouldn't judge your calling.[2]

Various views on leadership give us choices on what we want to be and how we want to act in our professional roles as fundraisers. Choices can also distort reality because these choices may represent stereotypes. Therefore, awareness and self-awareness are important in beginning to understand how fundraisers can become leaders—not necessarily leaders at the top, but leaders who are found at any rank and level.

This book is about awareness—understanding leadership and your own desire to become a leader from whatever position you hold. To begin, answer the following questions for yourself.

Think of a time when you experienced positive leadership. Why was this a positive experience? What characteristics or qualities (try to name at least five) did the leader exhibit that were the most important in making his or her leadership a positive experience for you?

As you develop your own strategy for leadership, you will want to begin with an understanding of the attributes, attitudes and habits that shape you.

First, who are you, as a fundraising professional? Have you always done what you've said you'd do? Are you seen as someone who tells the truth? Do you admit your mistakes? Do you have a reputation for hard work?

---

[2] Robert J. Lee and Sara N. King, Center for Creative Leadership, *Discovering the Leader in You: A Guide to Realizing Your Personal Leadership Potential* (San Francisco: Jossey-Bass, 2001), pp. 22–23.

While these characteristics don't necessarily make you a leader, they contribute to your successful practice of leadership.

Second, what do you know about your profession of fundraising? Have you done your homework? Do you know things others don't? Can you point to successful experience? On what basis do you introduce new facts or insights? A person lacking in knowledge is seldom acknowledged as a leader.

Third, how much of a fundraising professional are you? Do you listen well? Do you watch for nuances as well as statements? Are you sensitive to how others perceive you? More importantly, how do you perceive others—without biases or judgmental attitudes?

Fourth, how do you interact with people in any fundraising context? Do you tell people what to do, or are you good at getting their cooperation? Do you offer ideas as solutions or as the ultimate answers?

These questions are not exhaustive, of course, but perhaps they will help get you started in thinking about what it means to function in a leadership role, regardless of the formal role you hold in your organization.

In *Leadership from the Inside Out,* Kevin Cashman writes about the need to access not just our conscious beliefs, some of which we've

Self-knowledge and self-invention are lifetime processes. All the leaders I talked with agreed that no one can teach you how to become yourself, to take charge, to express yourself, except you. But there are some elements adopted by others that are useful to think about. I've organized them as the four lessons of self-knowledge. They are:

- *One: You are your own best teacher.*
- *Two: Accept responsibility. Blame no one.*

(continues)

- **Three:** *You can learn anything you want to learn.*
- **Four:** *True understanding comes from reflecting on your experience.*

—Warren Bennis[3]

addressed above, but also our shadow beliefs. The latter are those hidden, unexplored, or unresolved psychological dynamics and often are aspects we don't wish to examine. These, however, can be either strengths or weakness. Either way, they lead to consequences.[4] Competency in self-awareness is illustrated in Exhibit 1.1.

As self-awareness grows, it matures until a person acquires expertise in relationship management. This is important for the fundraiser, because our work is less about us than about everyone else, from donors to colleagues to community.

Added to the above questions, which identify self-awareness, is the awareness of leadership principles, competencies, and skills. Leadership literature is plentiful. Some is "pop" psychology; at the other end of the spectrum are the well-researched, scholarly theories. From Greek, Roman, and biblical times to the New Millennium, leadership has continued to fascinate and perplex. There are multiple definitions of leadership, as well as numerous theories about how leadership is developed—if, indeed, it can be. Although this book will bring in leadership theories, its main focus is on the practice of leadership and how it best supports the profession of fundraising.

---

[3] Warren Bennis, *On Becoming a Leader* (Reading, MA: Addison-Wesley, 1994), pp. 55–56.

[4] Cashman is quoted in Joe Raelin, "Preparing for Leaderful Practice," *Training and Development* (March 2004), p. 67.

EXHIBIT I.I   COMPETENCY IN SELF-AWARENESS

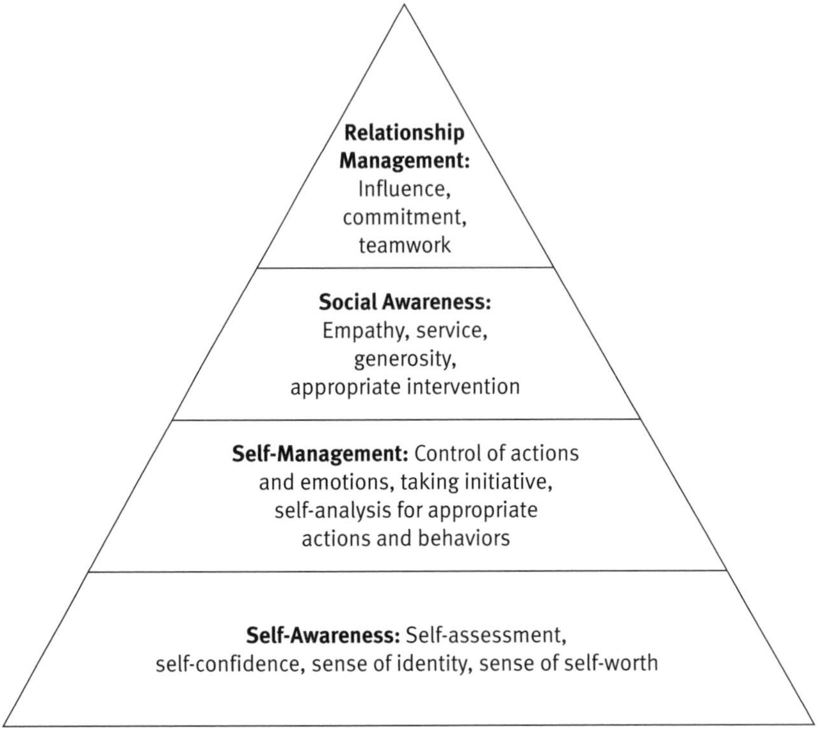

Relationship Management: Influence, commitment, teamwork

Social Awareness: Empathy, service, generosity, appropriate intervention

Self-Management: Control of actions and emotions, taking initiative, self-analysis for appropriate actions and behaviors

Self-Awareness: Self-assessment, self-confidence, sense of identity, sense of self-worth

Leadership can be present at all levels of an organization. Although structures and hierarchies exist, each individual can demonstrate and practice leadership competencies. According to James O'Toole, who wrote *Leadership A to Z: A Guide for the Appropriately Ambitious,* "Anybody at any level can help build leadership throughout the entire organization."[5] Therefore, this book contains what may be the best theories to help you discover how to develop your own style of fundraising leadership. These theories are used as bases for discussion as well as suggestions for leadership development.

---

[5] Haidee Allerton, "Leadership A to Z: An Interview with James O'Toole," *Training and Development* (March 2000), p. 58.

As you did earlier when considering questions about your leadership potential, style, and qualities, answer the following questions that relate to your awareness of a leadership knowledge base, particularly as it applies to your fundraising profession.

What is the latest book, book chapter, or article you have read about leadership? Was this a how-to piece, a descriptive item, or a theoretical work? What led you to choose this item to read? What did you gain from it? Could you summarize on one page your knowledge about leadership principles? Would you want more than a page?

There is something I know about you that you may not even know about yourself. You have within you more resources of energy than have ever been tapped, more talent than has ever been exploited, more strength than has ever been tested, and more to give than you have ever given.

—Stephen C. Lundin, Ph.D., Harry Paul, and John Christensen[6]

One of the newer concepts of leadership is described in the article "Wanted: Leader-Builders" by Steve Yearout, Gerry Miles, and Richard Koonce. The authors believe that leader-builders have these traits.

- An unusually strong vision of the future
- Remarkably consistent behaviors
- Strong emphasis on development and replenishment of the leadership talent pool

---

[6] Stephen C. Lundin, Ph.D., Harry Paul, and John Christensen, *Fish! A Remarkable Way to Boost Morale and Improve Results* (New York: Hyperion, 2000), p. 51.

- Identification of specific leadership competencies to support strategy

- Strong, strategic alignment

- A high degree of team unity

- Strong commitment to continuous organizational renewal[7]

These traits are particularly valuable for fundraising professionals, who truly must be leader-builders as they, their donors, their superiors, their constituents, and their peers work toward common goals. Subsequent chapters will look more specifically at the congruence between fundraising leadership and leadership traits.

In today's competitive and demanding climate, you need to start leading wherever you happen to be. In conclusion, perhaps Dorothy's adventure on the Yellow Brick Road is a good metaphor for how we can get things done when we're not ultimately in charge. In the classic story *The Wizard of Oz,* there are three main characters who befriend Dorothy and Toto. The first is the scarecrow. We can imagine this character saying, "I won't try to lead because I can't think." The second character is the cowardly lion who might say, "I haven't got any courage at all. I can't even scare myself . . . I'm afraid there's no denying it, I'm just a dandelion." The third is the tin man, who states, "Just to register emotion—if I only had a heart." Dorothy's friends typify some prevailing attitudes about leadership—the "I can't, I won't, I don't dare, I'm no good" statements. But through this little story we learn the one key factor that is the theme of this book. You can't always build a better boss, better board, better volunteers, but you can build a better YOU.

---

[7] Steve Yearout, Gerry Miles, and Richard Koonce, "Wanted: Leader-Builders," *Training and Development* (March 2000).

The wizard is you! Once you take the initiative, you are starting your own journey down the Yellow Brick Road toward building a better you—and, therefore, building a better you for fundraising leadership.[8]

REFLECTIONS

We're beginning to see that many of the tasks we need to perform in order to achieve our missions cannot be accomplished by following orders from just one person. All of us need to act and take a leadership role within our own domains. Consider the following case study, and reflect on how you might practice lateral leadership in coming to mutually satisfactory goals.

CASE HISTORY

John is chief development officer of a medical school foundation. The CEO of the foundation and CFO have met and discussed the budget, and John expected to be consulted about the amount of money he should raise. To his mild surprise, he sees the budget and finds out that the board has already approved it. He is to raise $3,750,000. John is concerned. He wanted to construct a gift range chart and discuss a realistic goal with his superiors. So, what should he do now?

- What are the issues involved?
- What options might John consider?
- What would be the best way to handle this situation?

---

[8] Adapted from Len Schlesinger, "It Doesn't Take a Wizard to Build a Better Boss," *Handbook of The Business Revolution* [Fast Company] (Hoboken: John Wiley & Sons, June 1996).

DEVELOP YOUR SKILLS

Reflect on what you read in this chapter about self-awareness and aware-ness of leadership principles. Consider the answers to these questions.

- Does your current or prospective position utilize what you believe you do well?
- Does it require leadership traits you have identified?
- Do you believe you have these traits? If not, what will you do to acquire and use them?

FOR FURTHER READING

Additional readings can be found at the end of the book.

Dean Anderson and Linda S. Ackerman Anderson. *Beyond Change Management: Advanced Strategies for Today's Transformational Leaders.* San Francisco: Jossey-Bass/Pfeiffer, 2001.

Geoffrey M. Bellman. *Getting Things Done When You Are Not in Charge: How to Succeed from a Support Position.* San Francisco: Berrett-Koehler, 1992.

Roger Fisher and Alan Sharp. *Getting It Done: How to Lead When You're Not in Charge.* Harper Business, 1998.

Garry Willis. *Certain Trumpets: The Call of Leaders.* New York: Simon & Schuster, 1994.

CHAPTER 2

Exploring Leadership:
Definitions and Dimensions

A survey of accepted concepts and tactics that guide the thinking and practice of leadership. These lay the groundwork for considering traits and characteristics that must be acquired for successfully leading from the middle.

More than 200 years ago, President Thomas Jefferson asked Meriwether Lewis to cross the Mississippi River to see if there was an all-river route to the Pacific Ocean. At that time, no one knew exactly how far the continent stretched or what type of terrain existed in the wilderness. Lewis chose his army buddy William Clark as his second-in-command. Both were in their early thirties. They set out in 1803 with 35 adventurers. Lewis had been a soldier, a plantation owner, and a personal secretary to President Jefferson, who spotted the leadership characteristics and charisma of the young man. Both Lewis and Clark exhibited leadership skills in accomplishing a bold and useful task.

- **They had to explore and chart unmapped territory.** Lewis spent two years acquiring scientific skills in order to do this.

- **They had to be optimistic, especially around others.** They faced physical and emotional stress during the expedition. The physical exertion would have strained the limits of any human.

- **They had to be courageous, not foolhardy.** They took risks but did so intelligently. Instead of attacking Native American tribes who were hostile, they learned to coexist. They never allowed pride to overshadow good judgment, and they remained focused on the enterprise at hand.

- **They were honest and objective.** Lewis was known for his proclivity for whiskey, but he also had the reputation for always being honest and objective. Jefferson said he had "a fidelity to truth so scrupulous that whatever he should report would be certain as if seen for ourselves."[1]

Lewis and Clark's leadership skills point out that many of our theories and principles about leadership are timeless. The roots of current leadership practice are based in ancient times and have shaped how we think about leadership today.

However, along the way, leadership knowledge has been tested and challenged, causing some principles to be modified or even discarded. This is an ongoing, dynamic process, and one that can cause discomfort to those who like the status quo. Most who strive to be leaders, however, are willing to put theories and practices into the appropriate context while moving ahead with new perspectives. Their attitude is probably exemplified by George Bernard Shaw, who wrote, "All progress is initiated by challenging current conceptions, and executed by supplanting existing institutions."[2] A playwright, critic, and social reformer

---

[1] Stephen Ambrose, Ph.D., "Inspiration: From Meriwether Lewis of Lewis & Clark Fame," *Bottom Line Personal* (September 1, 1996).

[2] George Bernard Shaw, as quoted in *Thoughts on Leadership* (Chicago: Triumph Books/The Forbes Leadership Library, 1995), p. 112.

who spanned the nineteenth and twentieth centuries, Shaw was known for being outspoken and for his barbed humor. His well-known play *Pygmalion* illustrates his desire to challenge status quo and bring about change. A stuffy intellectual and professor makes a bet that he can teach a low-class girl to speak and behave like a lady, and when he succeeds, the change is surprising to him and he unexpectedly falls in love with his new creation. Shaw probably would have approved of the changes in leadership theories that have occurred in recent years.

> *Letting go of the known in exchange for a commitment to the unknown is not something most human beings do comfortably or well.*
>
> —Karl Albrecht[3]

In similar ways, twenty-first century leadership theorists have done much to challenge conceptions and change their own and others' thinking about leadership. But without understanding the underpinnings of our knowledge of leadership, we can hardly move ahead in our professional growth as fundraisers, since we lack perspective. Where have we been? Where are we going? What do we want to achieve as leaders in our profession?

John W. Gardner, eminent professor, corporate leader, adviser to presidents, writer, and thought leader on leadership, wrote, "The first step is not action; the first step is understanding. The first question is how to think about leadership"[4] In *On Leadership,* a book that has

---

[3] Karl Albrecht, *The Northbound Train* (New York: AMACOM, 1994), p. 105.

[4] John W. Gardner, *On Leadership* (New York: The Free Press, 1990), p. xiv.

become a classic, Gardner wrote, "Leadership is the process of persuasion or example by which an individual (or leadership team) induces a group to pursue objectives held by the leader or shared by the leader and his or her followers."[5]

Gardner, while holding on to time-honored leadership principles and theories, also pointed the way to understanding how leadership works and distinguished leadership from status, power, and official authority. He listed nine tasks that he believed were the most significant functions of leadership: envisioning goals, affirming values, motivating, managing, achieving workable unity, explaining, serving as a symbol, representing the group, and renewing. Gardner was one of those at the forefront of thinking about how leadership means collaboration and motivation, especially in the nonprofit sector. However, he was preceded by a visionary who made startling statements for his time — Robert Greenleaf.

In 1970, Greenleaf, a retired AT&T executive, coined the term "servant-leadership" and launched a quiet revolution in the way in which we view and practice leadership. Greenleaf, in several writings on servant leadership,[6] refers to leaders as "affirmative builders of a better society." He claimed that a leader says, "I will go; come with me!" Servant-leadership, he wrote, involves others in decision making, is ethical behavior, demonstrates caring, and fosters individual growth within the context of organizational life.

This theory certainly stands in contrast to the hard-hitting expressions of approximately the same era, such as the one by Vance Packard, who wrote *The Pyramid Climbers*. Packard wrote, "Leadership appears

---

[5] *Ibid.*, p. 1.

[6] Cited throughout these texts are Robert K. Greenleaf, *Servant: Retrospect and Prospect* (Indianapolis, IN: The Robert K. Greenleaf Center, 1990), and Robert K. Greenleaf, *Servant Leadership: A Journey Into the Nature of Legitimate Power and Greatness* (New York: Paulist Press, 1977).

to be the art of getting others to want to do something that you are convinced should be done."[7] While Gardner spoke about the art of persuasion, Packard's ideas seemed to hark back to times when leadership was synonymous with power and was transacted from the top and nowhere else.

James M. Kouzes and Barry Z. Posner wrote that those who accept the leadership challenge must also challenge the process, because leadership is an active, not a passive process. Leaders are pioneers, they state, like Lewis and Clark—people who are willing to step into the unknown, to take risks, to innovate, to experiment, to find new and better ways of doing things, to recognize good ideas, to share a vision. They listed 10 commitments of leadership, most of which fit the role of fundraisers very well:

Challenging the Process

    1. Search for Opportunities

    2. Experiment and Take Risks

Inspiring a Shared Vision

    3. Envision the Future

    4. Enlist Others

Enabling Others to Act

    5. Foster Collaboration

    6. Strengthen Others

Modeling the Way

    7. Set the Example

    8. Plan Small Wins

---

[7] Quoted in James M. Kouzes and Barry Z. Posner, *The Leadership Challenge: How to Get Extraordinary Things Done in Organizations* (San Francisco: Jossey-Bass, 1987).

Encouraging the Heart

    9. Recognize Individual Contribution

  10. Celebrate Accomplishments[8]

> *Opportunity is missed by most people because it is dressed in overalls and looks like work.*
>
> —Thomas Edison[9]

Kouzes and Posner believe that leadership is not mystical and ethereal, something that can't be understood by ordinary people. "We have discovered hundreds of people who have led others to get extraordinary things done in organizations. There are thousands, perhaps millions, more. The belief that leadership cannot be learned is a far more powerful deterrent to development than is the nature of the leadership process itself."[10]

Few lives are filled with more historical significance than the life of Queen Elizabeth I, who reigned in the late sixteenth and early seventeenth centuries. She was a crafty ruler whose reign saw triumphs from literature (Shakespeare) to war (the Spanish Armada). The life of Queen Elizabeth has much to say for both those who are climbing the ladder to, perhaps, the top rung and those who are at the top and don't want to slip a rung. According to Alan Axelrod, the queen's long reign

---

[8] *Ibid.*, p. 14.

[9] Thomas Edison, quoted in Bill Jensen, *Simplicity: The New Competitive Advantage in a World of More, Better, Faster* (Cambridge, MA: Perseus Books, 2000), p. 108.

[10] Kouzes and Posner, *The Leadership Challenge*, p. 13.

offers numerous lessons in leadership.[11] Elizabeth treated England as a dynamic system based, perhaps, on certain unchanging, transcendent principles, but she was always responsive to the circumstances of a fluid world. She faced grave dangers, formidable challenges, and spectacular opportunities, and managed these both to her advantage and to that of England. She was an exceptional leader. She knew how to develop a leadership image, communicate effectively, establish priorities, inspire others, create loyalty and build a team, be an effective mentor, create maximum performance, and create exceptional quality.

Fundraisers probably don't think of a queen as an example of what they can do as leaders, but if we consider her five-centuries-old saga, we can see that she used time-tested leadership principles yet was not afraid to launch out and experiment, create, take risks, and hold on to her vision as she ruled her country. In the same way, fundraisers can adapt the principles shared and quoted in this book as exemplifying the acquisition of a knowledge base on which to build best practices of leading up.

Effective leadership combines individual traits and competencies with the demands of the situation in a particular group or organization. Most successful leaders adhere to group norms and demonstrate their leadership by helping the group achieve its goals. Effective leadership is the successful exercising of influence by the leader that results in goal attainment by the influenced followers. Leaders are agents of change, whose acts affect other people more than other people's acts affect them—leaders are not dictators who force others to do what they themselves want done. This was the belief of Ralph M. Stogdill, who died in 1978 and was Professor Emeritus of Management Sciences and Psychology at Ohio State. In 1981, Bernard M. Bass, Professor of

---

[11] Alan Axelrod, *Elizabeth I, CEO: Strategic Lessons from the Leader Who Built an Empire* (Paramus, NJ: Prentice Hall, 2000).

Organizational Behavior at State University of New York/Binghampton, wrote *Bernard M. Stogdill's Handbook of Leadership* in which he listed the essential leadership functions:

- Defining objectives and maintaining goal direction

- Providing means for goal attainment

- Providing and maintaining group structure

- Facilitating group action and interaction

- Maintaining group cohesiveness and group member satisfaction

- Facilitating group task performance

These traits are remarkably similar to those noted by later writers, such as David D. Chrislip and Carl E. Larson, who wrote *Collaborative Leadership—How Citizens and Civic Leaders Make a Difference*. They identified the skills for a new kind of leadership. They stated that the predominant forms of leadership are tactical, positional, and competitive. They suggest a new type, that of collaborative leadership. The primary role of collaborative leaders is to promote and safeguard the process. Four principles characterize collaborative leadership:

1. **Inspire commitment and action:** Collaborative leaders catalyze, convene, energize, facilitate others' creation of visions, and solve problems. They create new alliances, partnerships, and forums.

2. **Lead as peer problem solver:** Collaborative leaders do not do the work of the group for the group. Ownership of the process is shared. They are active and involved. Their role is to serve the group and the broader purpose for which it exists. They rely on credibility, integrity, and the ability to focus on the process.

3. **Build broad-based involvement:** They include a relevant community of interests. They include more people rather than fewer.

4. **Sustain hope and participation:** They convince participants that each person's input is valued, sustain confidence, and sustain commitment to the process.

Fundraising professionals can relate to the above principles because our work involves inspiring others and motivating their involvement in programs and organizations, solving problems as members of teams, and envisioning hope for a better future.

In a capstone publication of the Kellogg Leadership Studies Project (KLSP), a four-year enterprise that brought together leadership scholars and practitioners, Barbara Kellerman posed the following assumptions:

- Leaders matter—a lot.

- Followers matter as much.

- Leaders and followers working together can create change.

- Context matters—a lot (leadership can be studied historically and contextually, as well as ahistorically and acontextually).

- Globalization affects leadership—the information revolution, diversity, and the increasing divide between haves and have-nots, for example.

- Leadership is worth a lifetime of study—and then some.[12]

Fundraising is a challenging but meaningful profession. Fundraisers have to be part of the forward momentum, or they will be left floundering in the "but we've always done it that way" mentality. Our world needs fundraising leaders who can hold a competitive advantage and

---

[12] Barbara Kellerman, "Ringing Out the Old, Bringing in the New," in *Rethinking Leadership, Kellogg Leadership Studies Project* (College Park, MD: The Burns Academy of Leadership Press, 1998), p. 5.

have innovative ideas while holding on to time-tested principles. Knowing the difference between getting things done and getting things done better than ever is an art. Fundraising leadership from every level means being innovative, building on ideas and being adaptable, open to change, organized, entrepreneurial, and confident. Most of all, fundraising success demands that professionals know how to lead others toward a mutual vision.

Reflections

In an *Infoline* publication by ASTD Press,[13] Susan J. Thomas explains the concept of "thought leader. "Thought leaders are cutting-edge performers with innovative ideas who can move a group or discipline in a direction or to a point where it has not previously been. They have depth and breadth of knowledge in many areas and seek to influence events to get better outcomes."[14]

A self-assessment provided in the publication presents 20 questions to help determine if a person is ready to be a thought leader. Consider these five, adapted from the self-assessment, and respond "almost always," "most of the time," "some of the time," or "almost never."

1. I actively look for opportunities to learn something new.

2. I enjoy thinking "out of the box."

3. I synthesize idea from many sources to come up with new approaches.

4. I welcome change and new ways of doing things.

5. I actively encourage others to stretch, grow, and question.

---

[13] Susan J. Thomas, *Developing Thought Leaders, Infoline* 0410 (October 2004).

[14] *Ibid.*, p. 1.

If you answered "some of the time" or "almost never" for several of these, consider why you did so.

- Are you cautious, or inhibited in moving ahead?
- Have you been penalized for trying out new ideas?
- Can you balance your need for historical perspective and loyalty to tradition with the need to think innovatively and act courageously?

Develop Your Skills

Much of our education system teaches us to look for the one right answer. This works for many situations, but the danger is that if we believe we have the one right answer, we stop looking for alternative right answers.

"A leading business school did a study that showed that its graduates performed well at first, but in ten years, they were overtaken by a more streetwise, pragmatic group. The reason according to the professor who ran the study: 'We taught them how to solve problems, not recognize opportunities. When opportunity knocked, they put out their Do Not Disturb signs.'"[15]

Think back to a childhood riddle that may have intrigued you, such as this one. A man came to a river carrying a fox, a duck, and a bag of corn. There was a boat in which he could ferry one of the three items across the river at any one time. He could not leave the fox alone with the duck, nor the duck alone with the corn, so how did he get all three across? Remember playing with possible answers as you tried to solve riddles like this one?

---

[15] Roger Von Oech, *A Whack on the Side of the Head,* 3rd edition (New York: Warner Books, 1998), p. 31.

Now, think back on a puzzling, baffling, or frustrating situation you've had to handle in your fundraising career, maybe one like this:

CASE HISTORY

Susan is development director of a symphony in a city of about half a million population. On her organization's board are some well-connected people, because the symphony is the "chic" nonprofit to be involved with. She has a fundraising goal for the annual fund and needs to meet with volunteers. However, her CEO has made it clear that she must go through him before making any contact with the board. She is quite surprised, and asks if this is also true for the development committee and its chair. Yes, the CEO replies. So, Susan has a problem. How can she work with volunteers if she has no access to them?

- What three alternative solutions can you offer?
- Can you think of a fundraising dilemma you experienced, and in retrospect, offer more than one good, expected solution?

For Further Reading

Additional readings can be found at the end of the book.

Alan Axelrod. *Elizabeth I, CEO: Strategic Lessons from the Leader Who Built an Empire.* Paramus, NJ: Prentice Hall, 2000.

Joseph L. Badaracco, Jr. *Leading Quietly.* Boston: Harvard Business School Press, 2002.

John W. Gardner. *On Leadership.* New York: The Free Press, 1990.

John P. Kotter. "What Leaders Really Do." *Harvard Business Review* (December 2001), pp. 85–96.

CHAPTER 3

Leading in the
Real and Rough World

A reality check on fundraisers' roles and how they influence others from the middle. Through illustrations and facts, a common-sense approach to leadership will be addressed.

There is no simple formula that guarantees success as a leader. Leadership development requires dedication, self-motivation, a desire to learn, and experience. Learning to lead from any position or rank requires even more effort because it's not what we've been acculturated to do. Yet it's recognized as a vital leadership ability. Peter Drucker, a leading management guru, stated, "The [person] who focuses on efforts and who stresses his downward authority is a subordinate no matter how exalted his title and rank. But the [person] who focuses on contribution and who takes responsibility for results, no matter how junior, is in the most literal sense of the phrase, 'top management.'"[1]

---

[1] The author has substituted "person" in this quote for "man." Peter Drucker, *The Effective Executive* (New York: HarperCollins, 1993), p. 53.

James Burke, former chairman of Johnson & Johnson and leader of Partnership for a Drug-Free America, maintains that the hierarchical organization doesn't work anymore. He said, "The whole idea of hierarchical management with a general at the top and then several colonels comes out of the military and was transplanted into government as well as into business institutions. This pyramid organization never properly fit the needs of business, or any other institution."[2]

> *A good intention clothes itself with sudden power.*
>
> —Ralph Waldo Emerson[3]

Most leadership experts would agree that the hierarchy Burke talks about is dying because it was based on positional power—power that comes from several sources, including assigned, elected, appointed, usurped, grasped, and earned. Replacing this theory are other identifiable sources. For example, power is derived from relevance to company objectives. The position is significant, and the person in the position is central to success and not on the periphery. The person is a player, not a spectator. The professional has some degree of autonomy and can work independently within organizational parameters. There is visibility to colleagues and supervisors as well as to external constituents.

Charles Handy, who for many years taught at the London business school, stated that the "follow me" type of leadership was old fashioned,

---

[2] Lynne Joy McFarland, Larry E. Senn, and John R. Childress, *21st Century Leadership: Dialogues with 100 Top Leaders* (New York: The Leadership Press, 1993), p. 51.

[3] Ralph Waldo Emerson, *"The Conduct of Life,"* as cited in Joel Porte, ed., *Emerson: Essays and Lectures* (New York: The Library of America, 1983), p. 67.

and he coined a new term—distributed leadership. He used the analogy of a rowing crew who goes backward at high speed, without speaking to each other. Why does that work? An oarsman explained:

> In the race, on the job, it is the little person at the back of the boat, the one who can't row, who is in charge. He, or often she, is the task leader. But there is also the stroke, who sets the pace and the standard we all must follow. Off the river, however, the leader is the captain of the boat. He or she is responsible for choosing the crew, for our discipline, and for the mood and motivation of the group, but on the river the captain is just another member of the crew. Finally, there is the coach, who is responsible for our training and development. There is no doubt who is the leader when the coach is around.[4]

There isn't one leader, and the role shifts around, the rower explained.

Just as in the example of the rowing team, where leadership moves around, today's successful fundraising professional should practice distributed leadership. A development officer, as leader, helps crystallize goals and develops action plans to meet them. She is creative in designing development strategies, defining programs and projects, and employing methods and techniques particularly suited to the organization. Staff, volunteers, and donors must be motivated and inspired to action. The fundraising professional must be dedicated to purpose and to ongoing training and growth. As these and other functions work together, leadership is passed around and creates organizational change even in a chaotic environment that may be hostile to fundraising.

An analogy may be appropriate. In the life of a Native American tribe, the watercarrier held one of the most important and respected positions. Water, like food and air, is essential for survival. What does

---

[4] Frances Hesselbein, Marshall Goldsmith, and Richard Beckhard (eds.), *The Leader of the Future* (New York: The Drucker Foundation, 1996), p. 7.

The first basic ingredient of leadership is a guiding vision. The leader has a clear idea of what he wants to do—professionally and personally—and the strength to persist in the face of setbacks, even failures. Unless you know where you're going and why, you cannot possibly get there.

—Warren Bennis[5]

it mean to be a watercarrier for a modern-day nonprofit organization? Watercarriers bring commitment to their organizations, and that commitment extends to and strengthens the quality of an entire organization. Watercarriers transfer the essence of the institution to their colleagues, staff, superiors, constituents, donors, prospects, communities at large. Watercarriers help us see beyond the ephemeral.[6]

Fundraisers are the watercarriers of our day. The life of the organization often depends on their ability to exert appropriate leadership. The following represent only a sampling of what the watercarriers of nonprofit institutions must do:

- Examine, evaluate, and monitor the development program.
- Be alert to new situations.
- Seize opportunities.
- Keep abreast of trends and developments in the field.
- Seek to improve and refine the fundraising effort.
- Devote time to seeking major gifts.
- Identify, research, and evaluate prospects.
- Determine cultivation and communication efforts.

---

[5] Warren Bennis, *On Becoming a Leader* (Reading, MA: Addison-Wesley, 1994), p. 40.

[6] Adapted from Max De Pree, *Leadership Jazz* (New York: Dell, 1992).

- Be personally involved in solicitation.

- Work with the president and board.

- Develop leadership among volunteers.

- Identify new potential in leadership.

They must also ask and answer, in part, the following questions:

- Why are we what we are?

- What is important to us?

- What relationships are valuable and valued?

- Are we committed to problem solving?

- What legacy will we leave for our organization and its heirs?

- What is the need for community, internal, and external?

- Can we and do we manage change?

Today's climate for fundraising presents many challenges to the fundraiser and makes it necessary to note carefully how leadership traits can help us surmount these ever-present challenges.

For example, we must examine, evaluate, and monitor the development program so that we are able to meet agreed-upon or expected goals. This we must do while attending to pressures from donors, demands from superiors, and the desire for assistance from those whom we supervise, and also while we try to keep abreast of trends and developments in the field so that we and our organizations remain competitive. The pressures are many—demands for accountability, declining trust in nonprofit organizations, lack of trust that proper stewardship is practiced, lack of time, and an ever-ready media corps that watches our every move and is as prepared to criticize as publicize.

In accomplishing all this and more (and the tasks are well defined in a myriad of fundraising volumes), we find ourselves pressured to play many leadership roles. These are defined by Burt Nanus and Stephen M. Dobbs:[7]

- **The leader as visionary and strategist:** Nonprofit leaders move the organization in the right direction and work with others in the organization. They exemplify and share a vision for the common good.

- **The leader as politician and campaigner:** We must be spokespersons, advocates, and negotiators for the benefit of our organizations and constituents. And, we must also be superb fundraisers and campaigners for economic support.

- **The leader as coach:** Leaders are team builders. They create hope and confidence, they empower and inspire, they help others learn, grow, and realize their full human potential.

- **The leader as change agent:** Leaders position the organization for the future, make critical choices or influence others' decisions.

A leader in the nonprofit organization, such as a fundraiser, may need to be focused on one or more of the following directions:

- *Inside* the organization, where interaction takes place with board and volunteers, as well as staff, to inspire, encourage, enthuse and empower them.

- *Outside* the organization, where assistance is sought for support from donors, allies, the media, business leaders, and others.

- On *present* operations, where a leader is concerned about quality of service delivery, organizational structure, fundraising effectiveness, and information flow.

---

[7] Burt Nanus and Stephen M. Dobbs, *Leaders Who Make a Difference: Essential Strategies for Meeting the Nonprofit Challenge* (San Francisco: Jossey-Bass, 1999), pp. 18–19.

- On *future* possibilities, where a leader anticipates trends and developments that affect funding sources and income and, therefore, affect the future.[8]

In order to increase effectiveness, fundraisers must be aware of what is happening not only inside the organization but also outside its doors. This is called the Environmental Scan.[9] Albrecht lists eight basic environments, and while he describes these as external, for nonprofit organizations they have internal applications and implications as well (see Exhibit 3.1).

EXHIBIT 3.1   ENVIRONMENTAL SCAN

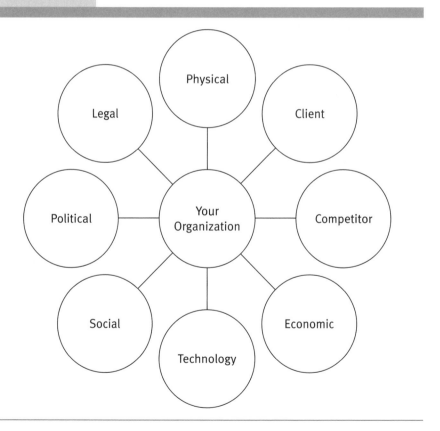

---

[8] Adapted from Nanus and Dobbs, *Leaders Who Make a Difference,* p. 17.

[9] Adapted from Karl Albrecht, *The Northbound Train* (New York: AMACOM, 1994).

Each of these aspects of the environment in which we as fundraisers work calls for leadership skills. We must know how to position ourselves so that we can be equal to or better than the competition, we need to be aware of how the economy and technological advances affect us, and we must adhere to our legal requirements and also manage political relationships, internally and externally. Of prime importance is our relationship to our clients and our ability to identify their wants, needs, values, and life situations and then determine how we can address these.

These demands made on fundraisers call for the requisites of true leadership, as Ron Heifetz wrote in *Leadership Without Easy Answers.* We must:

- Be able to identify challenges (gaps between aspiration and reality)
- Focus people's attention on those challenges
- Regulate level of distress by confronting issues
- Be capable of pacing the rate of change
- Keep attention focused on relevant issues
- Have poise and inner discipline
- Have courage[10]

Jeffrey Pfeffer, professor at Stanford University's Graduate School of Business, who has studied the use of influence and power, writes about what distinguishes those who achieve great influence from those who don't. His studies show that six characteristics make the difference:[11]

1. **Energy, endurance, and physical stamina:** Enables you to outlast the opposition, provides a role model, signals the importance of the task.

---

[10] Ronald Heifetz, *Leadership Without Easy Answers* (Cambridge, MA: Belknap Press of Harvard University, 1994).

[11] Jeffrey Pfeffer, "Six Characteristics of Leaders Who Influence Others Effectively," *The Nonprofit Board Report* (May 1993).

2. **Focus:** Keep your eye on the ball.

3. **Sensitivity to others:** This means understanding who are the people in your sphere of influence, what their positions on issues are, and how to best communicate with them.

4. **Ability to tolerate conflict:** Have a willingness to fight if necessary.

5. **Submerging one's ego:** Don't let your ego get in the way.

6. **Flexibility:** Change course if necessary and adopt new approaches to achieve goals.

Leadership is action. You act not only for yourself but also for the benefit of others. Therefore, fundraisers can and must exert leadership, because they are not working just for themselves but, more importantly, for the good of others.

REFLECTIONS

What challenges have you faced when trying to get things done when you didn't have the ultimate decision-making power? Do any of the following sound familiar?

- Your boss micromanages and gets involved in minute details.

- You don't get enough information about organizational programs or decisions and are caught off guard when talking with donors or board members.

- Your boss wants you to report on your weekly activities. This takes time, and you feel that he is checking on you.

- You go on solicitation calls out of town, and when you come back, your colleagues ask, "Did you have a good time?" They obviously don't understand fundraising!

- You aren't allowed access to the board, so you have difficulty motivating volunteers to become involved in fundraising.

DEVELOP YOUR SKILLS

Using the material provided for you in this chapter, determine what leadership traits are necessary for accomplishing the following "water-carrier" tasks.

Fund Raising Task (Not an exhaustive list)	Leadership Trait or Quality
Examine, evaluate, monitor development program	
Be alert to new possibilities for funding	
Keep abreast of trends and developments in the field	
Devote time to seeking major gifts	
Identify, train and work with volunteers	
Identify, research and evaluate prospects	
Determine cultivation and communication efforts	
Be personally involved in solicitation	
Work with the president and board	
Identify new potential in leadership	

FOR FURTHER READING

Additional readings can be found at the end of the book.

Peter F. Drucker. *The Effective Executive.* New York: HarperCollins, 1993.

John C. Maxwell. *The 21 Indispensable Qualities of a Leader.* Nashville, TN: Thomas Nelson, 1999.

Lynne Joy McFarland, Larry E. Senn, and John R. Childress. *21st Century Leadership: Dialogues with 100 Top Leaders.* New York: The Leadership Press, 1993.

Frances Hesselbein, Marshall Goldsmith, and Richard Beckhard, eds. *The Leader of the Future.* New York: The Drucker Foundation, 1996.

CHAPTER 4

Claiming Your Power to Change

Consideration of how to adapt and adopt principles for leading up. What mindset, attitude, and action changes must occur for successful leadership roles in fundraising.

The art of leadership, as well as individual practitioners of that art, are always works in progress," says Steven Sample, president of the University of Southern California. "They are never finished and complete; rather, they are always evolving, always changing, never static."[1] Sample further explains that a leader whose thinking is in a rut, who is governed by established passions and prejudices, who cannot use creative imagination, is as anachronistic and ineffective as the dinosaur—and his followers would be better off without him.

The need to change and adapt is further explained by Lynne Joy McFarland, Larry E. Senn, and John R. Childress, the authors of *21st Century Leadership.* They recommend that professionals take time out to reevaluate cherished beliefs and behaviors, to delete from their vocabulary

---

[1] Steven B. Sample, *The Contrarian's Guide to Leadership* (San Francisco: Jossey-Bass, 2002), p. 5.

the cursed phrase, "but we've always done it that way," and to accept that old skills may not work. "What we need is a new set of beliefs and behaviors, new technologies, and a fundamental shift in the relationship between leaders and their organizations."[2]

I don't know what your destiny will be, but one thing I know: the only ones among you who will be really happy are those who have sought and found how to serve.

—Albert Schweizer[3]

21st Century Leadership compiles the wisdom of 100 prominent leaders. One of these, Ray Smith, chairman and CEO of Bell Atlantic, states, "Everyone in an organization has an obligation to lead." Leadership is no longer the exclusive domain of the person on top, but a shared responsibility with appropriate roles accepted or assigned.[4] Rieva Lesonsky, editor-in-chief of *Entrepreneur Magazine,* is quoted as saying, "The biggest change in leadership is our perception of who can be a leader—and who can't be."[5] It used to be that political leaders and corporate magnates, all men, were considered leaders. That is no longer the case, and leadership is for everyone who accepts the responsibility and practices the principles, from kids to women to people from diverse cultures to men in traditional roles.

---

[2] Lynne Joy McFarland, Larry E. Senn, and John R. Childress, *21st Century Leadership: Dialogues with 100 Top Leaders* (New York: The Leadership Press, 1993), p. 184.

[3] Albert Schweizer, quoted in *Words of Wisdom for Writers, Speakers, and Leaders* (Silver Spring, MD: Philanthropic Service for Institutions, 1993), p. 127.

[4] McFarland et al., *21st Century Leadership,* p. 185.

[5] *Ibid.,* p. 187.

Can fundraisers accept this change in leadership practice and principles? Jay Conger, in a book on leadership training, asks the question, "Where do leaders come from?" Simply possessing leadership characteristics doesn't mean that someone will emerge as a leader. One must be motivated to lead—and want to learn how to lead, and, therefore, also adapt to changes and adopt new practices.[6]

"Leaders know that they need to be lifelong learners—school is never out. There is never one way, one system, one formula for doing something that is the end all and be all."

> Being a great employee isn't about "grinding" as much as it is about "soaring." We've already said that a great boss and a great employee want the same things—one, freedom; two, a change; and three, a chance. And by defining the great bosses, we have already defined the great employee. In fact, one of the joys of an alliance between two talented people is that the status distinctions fall away, the two merge.
>
> —Dale Dauten[7]

Part of the learning process is a challenge presented in the book *Fusion Leadership: Unlocking the Subtle Forces That Change People and Organizations.*[8] The authors maintain that there is a new way to lead,

---

[6] Jay A. Conger, *Learning to Lead: The Art of Transforming Managers Into Leaders* (San Francisco: Jossey-Bass, 1992).

[7] Elizabeth Jeffries, *The Heart of Leadership: Influencing by Design* (Dubuque, IA: Kendall/Hunt Publishing, 1992), p. 51

[8] Richard L. Daft and Robert H. Lengel, *Fusion Leadership: Unlocking the Subtle Forces that Change People and Organizations* (San Francisco: Berrett-Koehler, 2000).

based on the principles of "fusion," a joining together, rather than "fission," a splitting apart or separation. In the fission theory, there are rigid boundaries between followers and leaders; there is competition; information access and flow are limited; and layers of hierarchy and authority are used for control. The problems with this theory are that it limits ingenuity and creativity, and it causes inertia, which makes organizations resistant to change, or at least slow to respond to change.

Fusion, however, means the coming together and the creating of connections while reducing barriers. Conversation is encouraged, information is shared, and joint responsibility is assumed. A sense of community can therefore be created. The authors suggest that there are six forces that can bring about change in thinking and practice. Fundraisers should consider these seriously.

1. *Mindfulness* includes independent thinking, personal creativity, an open mind that welcomes novel and unusual ideas, and thinking outside the box.

2. *Vision* is the higher purpose toward which people work that provides meaning and inspiration for their collaborative efforts.

3. *Heart* represents caring and compassion, the positive feelings and emotions that underlie connections and relationships in the workplace.

4. *Communication* is the act of symbolically influencing others with respect to vision, values and emotions. Subtle communication also involves listening and discernment.

5. *Courage* is the motivation to step outside one's traditional boundary and comfort zone, to take risks, to take the lead, to be a nonconformist, to stand up for something, and to be willing to make mistakes as a way to learn and grow.

6. *Integrity* is honesty, trust, and service to others, which means going beyond "me, me, me" to give something to the team and the organization."[9]

Thinking about change can become overwhelming. Neuschel, writing in *The Servant Leader,* counsels that "If one is to survive and grow as a manager/leader, it is imperative that one identify the relatively few things that will make the greatest difference and then concentrate on them."[10] To set priorities, the fundraising professional should think in terms of end results and emphasize accomplishment, not activity, and discard the trivial and irrelevant.

It may help us to focus on adaptation and change if we look at the distinct areas that may be affected by our leadership. Exhibit 4.1 illustrates the concept of the parameters and complexities when leading up.

The key stakeholders may be the board and committees, other volunteers, community leaders, and other interested parties. In practicing leadership skills, you need to find out who these persons or groups are, what they value about the organization, and what their needs and expectations are.

- Donors are the lifeblood of our organizations. You need to determine how well their needs are met, what their potential giving is and what difference this will make to the organization, and how you can add to the donor pool.

- Corporate culture includes the structures of the organization, its culture and its values as well as its policies. You need to find out how the organization works in fulfilling its mission and relating to donors.

---

[9] *Ibid.,* p. 20–21.

[10] Robert P. Neuschel, *The Servant Leader: Unleashing the Power of Your People* (East Lansing, MI: Visions Sports Management Group, 1998), p. 75.

EXHIBIT 4.1   AREAS AFFECTED BY LEADERSHIP

EXHIBIT 4.1   AREAS AFFECTED BY LEADERSHIP

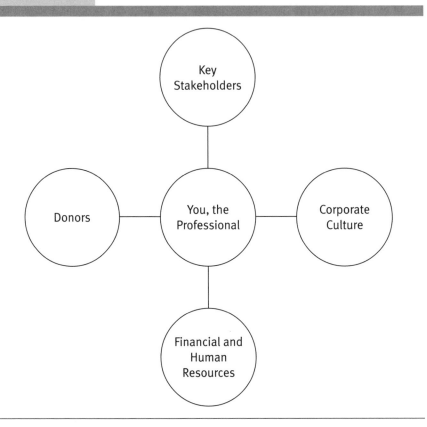

- Financial and human resources answer the questions of who will do what and how much it will cost. You need to determine if the resources are available and how effectively they are used.[11]

By nurturing the best qualities in each of the areas described above, we can lead up—we can motivate, influence, and change both ourselves and our organizations.

---

[11] Adapted from Burt Nanus and Stephen M. Dobbs, *Leaders Who Make a Difference: Essential Strategies for Meeting the Nonprofit Challenge* (San Francisco: Jossey-Bass, 1999).

Why is our leadership important? Because we manage through times of change, we can aid in determining direction, and we have a role in moving organizations from where they are to where they want to be. By our own example, we can shape the corporate culture. By using the best management tools, we can ensure that resources are wisely used. Most of all, we can mobilize support and encourage others to do the same.[12]

The ultimate challenge is not only understanding leadership traits but also knowing how to use them in our communication with our supervisors and others to whom we report so that we can gain support for our fundraising programs. We must think about "leading up." Based on the concepts of John Dewey, the pioneering educational theorist, as well as organizational management specialists, Mary Lippitt identifies six types of leadership and discusses the decision-making priorities of each.[13] The leader types she identifies are:

1. **The Inventor,** who develops new ideas, products and services.

2. **The Catalyst,** who wants to gain the market share and acquire customers.

3. **The Developer,** who builds infrastructure and creates systems and processes for high performance.

4. **The Performer,** who improves processes and procedures for effective use of resources.

5. **The Protector,** who cherishes values and develops a committed workforce, builds capabilities, a supportive culture, and a positive identity.

---

[12] Adapted from Noel M. Tichy with Eli Cohen, *The Leadership Engine: How Winning Companies Build Leaders at Every Level* (New York: HarperCollins, 1997).

[13] Mary Lippitt, "How to Influence Leaders," *Training and Development* (March 1999).

6. **The Challenger,** who identifies strategic options and positions the organization for the future.

These characteristics will be useful as we continue to seek self-awareness, but they also increase our understanding of how we can best interact with others who exhibit these priorities in decision making and in taking action.

Finally, we must remember that change is gradual, and we will adapt only if we are convinced that it's imperative for our professional and personal success. It's up to us to make that difference. The story of Rebecca Lukens perhaps illustrates this concept best. In the early 1800s, Rebecca and her husband took over a small water-driven iron mill that made nails, located next to the Brandywine Creek in rural Pennsylvania. They had big plans to build up their small business, but before their expansion plans could get under way, Rebecca's husband died, leaving her at the age of 31 with four young children and a fifth on the way. She could have sold her interest in the mill and merely played the expected role of homemaker. But due partly to a promise she'd made to her dying husband, and in spite of severe financial strain, she took over management of the ironworks herself. She had made up her mind that their dream was achievable, and she knew that "If it is to be, it is up to me."

Rebecca Lukens was equal to the challenge in every way. She carried through with the expansion plans, enlarging the mill and the product line to include plate iron. She provided the iron hull and boiler plates for the Navy's first iron ship in 1825. Many of the Mississippi river boats came to rely on Lukens' ironwork for their boilers. For thirty years she dauntlessly managed the business, surviving a severe economic depression, developing her company into one of the nation's major ironworks of that era, and she did all this in what was then a man's world with a man's kind of business. Today, Lukens Steel is a leading company, built by a can-do tradition handed down from its remarkable early leader, in whose honor it is named.

In the same way, fundraising professionals provide this kind of vision and combine it with a determination of "if it is to be, it's up to me" to appropriately challenge others, to motivate, to influence, to inspire, and to ensure that our organizational mission is sustainable because we have the courage to practice leading up.

REFLECTIONS

Imagine that you are about to be interviewed by someone of the caliber of Tom Brokaw, Barbara Walters, or another current luminary in the news business. This person is doing a documentary on leaders who build organizations by practicing good leadership skills. In 60 seconds the camera is coming on you. At that point the interviewer will say to you, "Please tell me your views on leadership and how you lead in your organization." How will you respond to this interview question?

_____

_____

_____

_____

You may wish to share your answer with someone else to see how well you were able to articulate your views on leading from the middle, or leading up, or lateral leadership.

DEVELOP YOUR SKILLS

This is an exercise on how to influence leaders. We may need to "lead up," which means getting support for our ideas and programs. We are partners with our leaders, and, therefore, must be sources of information and recommendations. The following are the types of decision-making leaders, the questions that determine their priorities, and the priorities that are characteristic of each type of leader. We are leaders as well, and fit into these categories. After reading the first three columns, determine what type of leader you might be. This questionnaire is adapted from Mary Lippitt's article, "How to Influence Leaders" in *Training and Development,* March 1999.

Type of Decision-Making Leader	Questions Asked to Determine Priorities	Priorities for Type of Leader	Your Type
Inventor	What is the latest thinking? What's possible?	Developing new ideas, products and services	
Catalyst	What can help us compete? What do our clients and donors want?	Gaining market share and acquiring customers	
Developer	How can we improve or clarify roles and responsibilities? What systems can leverage our resources and talents?	Building and infrastructure and creating systems and processes for high performance	
Performer	How can we do it better? How can we become more efficient?	Improving processes and procedures for effective use of resources	
Protector	How can we develop talent? How can we develop a supportive environment?	Developing a committed workforce, building capabilities, supporting culture, identity, values	
Challenger	What opportunities are there? How can we prepare for the future?	Identifying strategic options and positioning the organization for the future	

FOR FURTHER READING

Additional readings can be found at the end of the book.

Joseph L. Badaracco, Jr. *Leading Quietly.* Boston: Harvard Business School Press, 2002.

Donald T. Phillips. *Lincoln on Leadership.* New York: Warner Books, 1992.

Wess Roberts. *Leadership Secrets of Attila the Hun.* New York: Warner Books, 1987.

Robert Slater. *Get Better or Get Beaten! 29 Leadership Secrets from GE's Jack Welch.* New York: McGraw-Hill, 2001.

Noel M. Tichy with Eli Cohen. *The Leadership Engine: How Winning Companies Build Leaders at Every Level.* New York: HarperCollins, 1997.

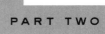

PART TWO

Leadership Traits and Characteristics and Their Applicability to Fundraising

CHAPTER 5

"Them and Us"

*Fundraisers share the challenge of working with people
and processes that move the organization toward its primary
mission. Most of us do this from the middle, not the top,
of "corporate" pyramids. "Them" and "Us" is not meant to
be adversarial but to indicate the differences between those
who have designated power and identified leadership status,
and us who those lead up, from whatever position we hold.[1]*

John Gardner, a respected thinker on leadership, once spoke to a group of community leaders and shared his thoughts about the true concept of leadership:

> Years ago, Dwight Eisenhower said to me that the heart of combat leadership in the military services is the noncommissioned officer; and most military people share his view. It is ironic that we think of military people as wholly preoccupied with top brass, when it is we civilians who are truly fascinated with our topmost leaders, giving little thought to the middle-level and lower-level leadership so crucial to our system.[2]

---

[1] Adapted for fundraisers from Geoffrey M. Bellman, *Getting Things Done When You Are Not in Charge* (San Francisco: Berrett-Koehler Publishers, 1992), p. 5.

[2] John W. Gardner, "Exploring Leadership," Remarks to the National Association of Community Leadership Organizations (September 9, 1984).

Gardner was right, and the views he decried have lasted until today, although we've become somewhat more open-minded about where leadership originates and how it is practiced. We still place much attention on and hold respect for those in designated positions of power, while giving little attention to true leadership that comes from many sources.

Gardner went on to say that "the manner in which we have spread power and initiative in our society opens the way to a dispersed leadership that could vitalize every part and every level of our society." He was optimistic that in our culture, based on democratic values, leadership would extend beyond the top, positional power.

Many of us who are fundraisers see ourselves in jobs that primarily support the success of others or of organizations. We view ourselves as being in service positions—in service to our bosses and boards, donors and volunteers, communities and clubs. Our perspective, therefore, becomes one of looking up from a subservient position, as exemplified by "them" and "us."[3]

In an amusing book with a serious message, *Throwing the Elephant: Zen and the Art of Managing Up,* author Stanley Bing equates bosses in positions of power to elephants. He points out that many infractions of law, ethics, and business have been the practice of the elephants in our midst. They make the messes, and they can do so because they are elephants, one and all. Who is going to clean up the messes? "The elephant? Ha! No such thing. Wrap your no-mind around it. Most of your activity, particularly in the beginning of your time in service, will take place behind the elephant. They do their thing or, at times, things. We clean up after them. That is the law of nature, or at least of elephants."[4]

---

[3] Adapted for fundraisers from Geoffrey M. Bellman, *Getting Things Done When You Are Not in Charge* (San Francisco: Berrett-Koehler Publishers, 1992), p. 14.

[4] Stanley Bing, *Throwing the Elephant: Zen and the Art of Managing Up* (New York: HarperBusiness, 2002), p. 46.

Lincoln was not great because he was born in a log cabin, but because he got out of it.

—James Truslow Adams[5]

This attitude can be pervasive among fundraisers. Consider, for example, if you can recognize yourself in at least some of these statements:

- We have expertise, but usually someone else has the authority.

- We don't make the final decision; if we're lucky, we influence the decision.

- We work with people who have more clout than we do— financial, decision making, political, and social.

- Our roles are viewed differently by different people. Our most important role, providing institutional support, isn't always recognized or understood.

- Our reputation as individuals and members of a profession may not be as valued as that of doctors, lawyers, or professors. But our function often helps them to be successful.

- Users of our services often see us as less important, subordinate, or peripheral. We are tolerated, maybe even respected, but not fully valued.

David Chrislip and Carl Larson have examined the two predominant forms of leadership in our culture. These are tactical and positional

---

[5] James Truslow Adams, quoted in Forbes Magazine, *Thoughts on Leadership* (Chicago: Triumph Books/The Forbes Leadership Library, 1995), p. 114.

leadership.[6] Both of these propagate the "them" and "us" culture under which we often work.

Tactical leadership is often defined by metaphors—win the game, defeat the enemy, apprehend the suspect. As the term "tactical" implies, much depends on a plan for achieving an objective, and people are led in an effort to accomplish the plan. Tactical leaders can be coaches, military leaders, film directors, presidents of colleges. In this kind of leadership, a clearly identified leader—who may have assumed the position in a number of ways ranging from force to mutual consent by the members—may set the goal, convince us that we must work to achieve that goal, organize and strategize, and deal with us as part of the effort to reach the goal.

Positional leadership identifies someone at the top of the organizational structure. This leader is in charge of an organization, unit or other type of structure, and in many ways, is similar to the tactical leader. The purpose is to perform a set of tasks or activities.

These types of leadership are often ingrained in us. Our presidents or executive directors, our boards, and the vice presidents or directors of development, all tell us what to do, and, usually, how to do it. We are judged by how we perform according to the set goals and standards. This reinforces the concepts of "them" versus "us."

In view of these beliefs and theories, we have to make an effort to realize we share the challenge of working with people and processes that move the organization toward its primary mission. Although most of us do this from the middle, not the top, of "corporate" pyramids, we do play roles in determining the organization's strategic direction, and we are essential for getting results. Our ultimate purpose should be to serve in the achievement of others' goals and purposes, while simultaneously reaching for our own.

---

[6] David D. Chrislip and Carl E. Larson, *Collaborative Leadership — How Citizens and Civic Leaders Can Make a Difference* (San Francisco: Jossey-Bass, 1995).

Our perceptions of "them" versus "us" are often defined in negative ways, leaving us as fundraisers in subordinate positions, especially in the perceptions of those whom we must influence and lead.

Them	Us . . . .
Pride themselves in action for results	Provide the source of the action
Focus on the core mission of the organization	Support the mission by ensuring financial support and the goodwill of the community
Decide	Have to live with the decision
Have many resources reporting to them	Have few resources, and at times have to struggle to obtain them
Are concerned with the bottom line	Contribute to the bottom line through our work to support the top line (mission)

This list could go on, and later we'll ask you to put it into a personal context. How you view "them" versus yourself and your role has a lot to do with your current leadership style, if indeed you have acquired one, and your potential to be an effective leader.

Many of us are fundraising managers, and good ones at that, but lacking in leadership traits. Leaders must manage, and managers must lead, but the two are not synonymous.

Management means getting things done with and through others, which requires leadership skills and the ability to relate to others. For example, look at the characteristics of management and leadership:

Managing Is	Leading Is . . . .
Working within boundaries	Expanding boundaries
Planning and goal setting	Creating a vision
Getting the work done	Committing to getting the work done no matter what

(continues)

(Continued)

Managing Is	Leading Is . . . .
Measuring performance	Assessing accomplishment
Attention to detail	Attention to the big picture
Setting direction	Planning and budgeting
Aligning people	Organizing and staffing
Motivating people	Controlling and problem solving
Working with available resources	Influencing others

According to John P. Kotter, "leadership and management are two distinctive and complementary systems of action. Each has its own function and characteristic activities. Both are necessary for success in an increasingly complex and volatile business environment."[7] Management, he says, is about coping with complexity. Leadership, on the other hand, is about coping with change.

If at this point you're saying, "But traits from both columns are required for success," then you are correct. Regardless of a person's position in the fundraising department of an organization, success requires skills from both management and leadership. The problem is that fundraising professionals are often so busy and overburdened with work that they forget to practice the leadership traits that will take them to greater success, such as motivating volunteers, influencing decision making based on rational facts, and empowering organizational leaders (defined by position) to accept their appropriate roles. Peter Drucker expressed the importance of being both a good manager and leader in this way:

> These roles of modeling principle-centered leadership—path-
> finding, aligning, and empowering—represent a paradigm that is

---

[7] John P. Kotter, "What Leaders Really Do," *Harvard Business Review* (December 2001), p. 85.

different in kind from traditional management thinking. There is a very significant difference between management and leadership. Both are vital functions and because they are, it's critical to understand how they are different so one isn't mistaken for the other. . . . Leadership focuses on doing the right things; management focuses on doing things right. Leadership makes sure the ladders we are climbing are leaning against the right wall; management makes sure we are climbing the ladders in the most efficient ways possible.[8]

The concept of "them" versus "us" will persist if we don't begin to understand and accept that new leadership skills and behaviors, new followership skills and behaviors, and new interaction between the two parties is the responsibility of both the acknowledged leaders and those leading up. Change must take place, both in yourself and in the way you practice leadership skills to help implement change in your organization.

Some of the most commonly held beliefs about formal leaders are inhibitors, such as these:

- They have to be role models for change.

- They have to practice what they preach, or "walk the walk and talk the talk."

- They must implement change.

- They should have conquered their imperfections and mistakes and have dealt with their inadequacies.

- They must support our work through adequate resources.

- They must understand what we do and support it.

These beliefs and the subsequent attitudes demand perfection from leaders and put us into a subordinate position—a stereotype of the

---

[8] Frances Hesselbein, Marshall Goldsmith, Richard Beckhard (eds.), *The Leader of the Future* (New York: The Drucker Foundation, 1996).

Good leadership consists of motivating people to their highest levels by offering them opportunities, not obligations.

That is how things happen naturally. Life is an opportunity and not an obligation.

—John Heider[9]

"them" and "us" syndrome. We can overcome these stereotypes by becoming innovators and accepting challenges, always with our bosses' knowledge and their blessing; being self-managers and understanding our own roles, identities, and possibilities; and taking appropriate, calculated, knowledgeable risks.

When we understand that we are not in charge, and if we were, things might not be that much different because of the nature of the organization and its environmental influence, we can begin to develop leadership traits that lead to "leading up." We can:

- Appreciate our uniqueness, valuing, emphasizing, and using our best skills and letting our positional leaders understand how these help the organization succeed.

- Be self-confident about our expertise and effort, appropriately taking credit when goals are reached, yet sharing the credit with all members of the team.

- Be open to and manage change within our own departments and programs, thereby showing that we will accept greater change in the organization.

---

[9] John Heider, *The Tao of Leadership: Lao Tzu's Tao Te Ching Adapted for a New Age* (New York: Bantam Books, 1986), p. 135.

Much of this, and more, is the thinking of leadership experts in the twenty-first century. The concepts and ideas aren't necessarily new—what is new is the increasing emphasis on collaborative leadership, on the concept of leading up, on being flexible and adaptive, and on discarding attitudes, beliefs, and skills that just don't work any more.

In a booklet on the leadership edge, published by the American Society of Association Executives, the seven skills of the twenty-first century leader were enumerated. All of these are appropriate for the fundraiser to consider:

1. **Servant Leadership:** True leadership begins with the desire to serve others. Fundraisers do not work for their own benefit but for the good of the client and all other constituents.

2. **Creating and Communicating Vision:** Fundraisers create a compelling vision of the future as they raise funds to support that vision, and they must be able to communicate that vision internally and externally, to all constituents.

3. **Promoting and Initiating Change:** Fundraisers advocate and initiate change that recreates the organization in response to a constantly changing environment.

4. **Building Partnerships:** Individual competence, worthy as it is for the fundraiser, is not enough. Alliances and partnerships will build the strength of the organization and the professional.

5. **Valuing Diversity:** Demographics and geographical barriers are breaking down, and dealing with diversity of every kind is not only necessary but a strengthening factor in competing for financial support.

6. **Managing Information and Technology:** The welter of information is boundless, and the fundraiser must learn how to manage information, avoid overload, and keep human needs and concerns in balance with technology.

7. **Achieving Balance:** The fundraiser can easily become overwhelmed by demands from the "them" element and forget to keep a balance in his or her own needs.[10]

When there is no leadership . . .

Nobody listens. Nobody pays attention.

   People stop doing good work.

Teamwork disintegrates.

   The workplace gets nasty.

People pick on each other.

   Quality goes out the window.

Some employees quit and leave.

   Some employees quit and stay.

Customers (donors) leave . . . often in a hurry!

   Business dries up.

—John Baldoni[11]

Perhaps the best way to remember how to overcome the "them" versus "us" dilemma, which can limit our vision, hamper our activity, squelch our enthusiasm, and reduce us to whimpering nonentities is to practice the five "A's" of leadership. Be:

1. **Approachable:** Listen to what others have to say. Make yourself accessible to others, and invite them to talk about whatever is on their minds. Even bosses need someone to listen to them!

---

[10] Sheila Murray Bethel, *Beyond Management to Leadership: Designing the 21st Century Association* (Washington, DC: Foundation of the American Society of Association Executives, 1993).

[11] John Baldoni, *180 Ways to Walk the Leadership Talk* (Dallas, TX: The Walk the Talk Company, 2000).

2. **Accepting:** Keep an open mind. Good ideas can come from everyone, and the best ones sometimes come from those who aren't seen as leaders. Sometimes that might even be you. If you've accepted others' ideas, yours will have a chance of being accepted.

3. **Acknowledging:** Recognize the contributions of others. Thank someone every day, including your boss, board chair, volunteers, colleagues, donors. . . .

4. **Accountable:** Be responsible for yourself and the actions of others under your charge. Be accountable on behalf of the institution and its mission.

5. **Adaptable:** Change is inevitable and often is welcome. Think about where your organization and your donors want and need to be in the future, and make adjustments for how to get there.[12]

Change is inevitable; progress is optional.

—David Sternberg, *The Fund Raising School*

As we who practice the noble profession of fundraising internalize the five "A's," we will be able to move beyond a mentality of "us" and "them" and toward the less-threatening, more comfortable, ultimately positive, and definitely productive stance of "we."

---

[12] Adapted from John Baldoni, *180 Ways to Walk the Leadership Talk* (Dallas, TX: The Walk the Talk Company, 2000).

REFLECTIONS

What is the most meaningful thing you have done in the past week for your fundraising program and its success? Jot this down, then answer the following questions:

- Why was it important?
- Why was what you wrote important?
- Why was what you wrote above important?

Keep answering that question until you have just one word left. Think about the ultimate reason why you are a fundraiser. Think about how you can provide leadership so that what you do is important not just to you, but to your organization and its service to clients and donors.

DEVELOP YOUR SKILLS

Assess your attitude about your leadership potential. Answer "yes," "no," "sometimes," or "maybe."

- Do you believe you are a powerless player in a game managed by someone else?
- Do you leave thinking and responsibility for the future to others and focus on your daily work?
- Do you react more than act, and follow orders without thinking?
- Do you experience strong emotions about work that aren't positive (for example, blame, resentment, anger) without trying to figure out where they are coming from?
- Are you reluctant to act on your ideas because of fear of failure?

If you answered "yes" or "sometimes" to most of these, then you are entrenched in the "them" versus "us" syndrome. Consider a shift to a new way of thinking.

- Become more aware of what you think and feel and what influences you. Then consider how you can influence ideas, options, and actions.

- Understand your feelings and reactions—of all kinds. Explore what you need to do to assume a position and attitude of leadership.

- Treat others as partners, understand and appreciate all roles, and consider yourself a worthy member of the team.

Our beliefs create ourselves and our world. Make those beliefs count for something great.

FOR FURTHER READING

Additional readings can be found at the end of the book.

Robert J. Lee, Sara N. King, and the Center for Creative Leadership. *Discovering the Leader in You: A Guide to Realizing Your Personal Leadership Potential.* San Francisco: Jossey-Bass, 2001.

John C. Maxwell. *The 21 Irrefutable Laws of Leadership.* Nashville, TN: Thomas Nelson, 1998.

John P. Schuster. "Transforming your Leadership Style." *Association Management,* Washington, vol. 46, issue 1 (January 1994), p. 39.

CHAPTER 6

A Model for a
New Kind of Leader

A visual perspective often helps us understand concepts.
This chapter illustrates the concepts of leading up, or lateral
leading, through a model developed by the authors.

In 1970, Scott Myers wrote *Every Employee a Manager,*[1] in which he argued that organizations would be best served if all employees were treated as managers.

Since that time, many authors, experts, researchers, and thought leaders have extrapolated Myers's idea to mean that leadership development can and should take place at every level of an organization. Of course, there are differences in assignments and responsibilities at the various ranks and positions, but leadership, as we have seen, can take place at any level.

Sandra Trice Gray, formerly in charge of leadership programs at Independent Sector in Washington, DC, wrote that the twenty-first century leader must stay alert and view change as an opportunity. Gray outlined

---

[1] Scott Myers, *Every Employee a Manager* (New York: McGraw-Hill, 1970).

what she called a new set of rules for leadership. According to Gray, the twenty-first century leader:[2]

- No longer believes that to give away power is to lose something.
- Possesses a global and holistic perspective.
- Creates and communicates vision.
- Employs strategic thinking.
- Promotes and initiates change.
- Embraces and values diversity and inclusiveness.
- Manages technology and distributes information.
- Inspires, motivates, and stimulates, leading through personal persuasion and valuing emotions as well as ideas.
- Models integrity and ethical behavior, obeying unenforceable and self-imposed laws.
- Integrates an ongoing system of evaluation, creating more open, effective, empowered, and excellent organizations.
- Respects and values people with support, understanding, care and empathy.

James MacGregor Burns presents the following definition in his classic book Leadership: *Leadership is the reciprocal process of mobilizing, by persons with certain motives and values, various economic, political, and other resources, in a context of competition and conflict, in order to realize goals independently or mutually held by both leaders and followers . . . Leaders can also shape and alter and elevate the motives and values and goals of followers through the vital teaching role of leadership. This is* transforming leadership.[3]

---

[2] Adapted from Sandra T. Gray, "Fostering Leadership for the New Millennium," *Leadership* (1995).

[3] James MacGregor Burns, quoted in *Leadership IS* (March 1995), p. 60.

In looking at our profession of fundraising in the twenty-first century, a leadership definition that seems most suitable is the one by Independent Sector: "Leadership is an activity or set of activities, observable to others, that occurs in a group, organization, or institution involving a leader and followers who willingly subscribe to common purposes and work together to achieve them."[4] In fleshing out this definition, the Independent Sector publication *Leadership IS* first provides a historical context for development of leadership records, literature, and research, then summarizes the dimensions of leadership. Two basic leadership dimensions, performance and maintenance, are classic descriptions of leadership behaviors, but many believe additional dimensions are necessary for organizational effectiveness. Some of these are:

- **Support:** Behavior that enhances someone else's feeling of personal worth and importance.

- **Interaction facilitation:** Behavior that encourages members of a group to develop satisfying relationships;

- **Goal emphasis:** Behavior that stimulates an enthusiasm for meeting group goals or achieving excellence in performance

- **Work facilitation:** Behavior that helps in attaining goals through planning and action.[5]

From the many theories presented, the following dimensions perhaps encompass the fundraiser's practices the best:

- Informing

- Consulting and delegating

- Planning and organizing

---

[4] Kenneth E. Clark and Miriam B. Clark, "Definitions and Dimensions of Leadership," in *Choosing to Lead,* reprinted by permission in *Leadership IS* (1994).

[5] *Ibid.,* p. 68.

- Problem solving

- Clarifying roles and objectives

- Monitoring operations and environment

- Motivating

- Recognizing and rewarding

- Supporting and mentoring

- Managing conflict

- Team building

- Networking[6]

With these dimensions in mind, along with the information that has been presented in prior chapters, which describe leadership characteristics and traits, the following model can serve as a catalyst as well as anchor for our thinking about leading up!

The fundraising professional has to manage two sets of requirements. One of these is organizational leadership. These tasks range from simple to complex. The organization has:

- *Policies,* which must be managed.

- *Meetings,* which must be organized, attended, and led.

- *Records,* which must be accurate, must be kept in good order, and are subject to review by external parties.

- *Routine maintenance procedures,* which must be handled (that is, program and procedure maintenance).

- *Budgets,* which must be developed, followed, and audited.

- *Communication flow,* which must produce optimal information to support decision-making and day-to-day management.

---

[6] *Ibid.,* p. 69.

- *Constituent relations,* which must ensure that clients needs are met, while maintaining good relationships with all external groups to ensure public awareness, trust, and a positive organizational image.

These are just the highlights of what it takes to for an organization to function effectively.

As an employee and member of the team, a fundraiser shares in the responsibilities of organizational leadership. Some of these may be:

- Developing appropriate committees for internal advice on fundraising
- Conducting information meetings
- Keeping top assigned leaders informed and involved
- Being accountable for resources, internally and externally
- Keeping accurate records and producing timely, informative reports
- Managing personnel, if that is part of the job description
- Maintaining good communications across departments as well as the organization

In accomplishing these tasks, the fundraising professional must often employ excellent leadership skills, since he or she is probably not at the top of the management pyramid, where the fulfillment of these responsibilities is expected. Here's where Gardner's leadership traits, for example, are good resources. As cited in Chapter 2, he listed nine tasks that he believed were the most significant functions of leadership: envisioning goals, affirming values, motivating, managing, achieving workable unity, explaining, serving as a symbol, representing the group, and renewing.

The model in Exhibit 6.1 shows the dimension of organizational leadership and illustrates how the tasks of fundraising leadership can

EXHIBIT 6.1   LEADERSHIP MODEL

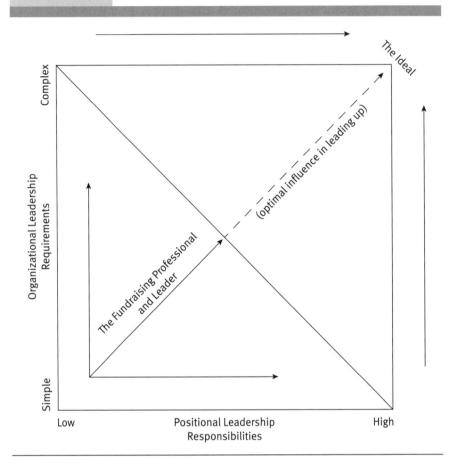

range from the simple to the complex, and must be accomplished at least at the minimum level to achieve satisfying performance. Going beyond the dimension, symbolized by the diagonal line between "complex" and "high," means that the professional has grasped the concepts and ideals of leading up and has moved beyond the rudimentary fulfillment of duties and expectations.

Looking at the other dimension of the model, Positional Leadership Responsibilities, we can outline the specific tasks that a fundraising professional must accomplish.

- **Direct mail or direct marketing:** This includes producing and distributing written materials to a targeted audience. Some particular skills and qualifications needed are writing, the ability to work with a deadline, willingness to seek advice from other professionals, creativity, and technical expertise. A professional must have the ability to handle lists, sometimes of great length, write copy, handle the details of getting a mailing out, and produce reports on the results.

- **Special events:** This consists of organizing functions or benefits that meet several goals, from cultivation and creating good will to raising funds. The skills and qualifications needed include organizational ability, the ability to manage many details, creativity in selecting a type of event, and the ability to work well with volunteers. Certainly a great deal of patience and flexibility are required in this area.

- **Prospect research:** This consists of finding appropriate information about prospects and donors, and managing this information. This subspecialty has taken on new dimensions with the growth of technology. The person undertaking research must be able to do so by using the Internet as well as many other resources, maintain records on computer software, compile information, record and manipulate data, and support staff, volunteers, and administrators with appropriate information.

- **Major donor solicitation:** This consists of working with people who have the capacity to make large gifts to the organizations. A person specializing in this area must be able to identify and qualify major gift prospects, plan a strategy for cultivation and solicitation, often ask for the gift, provide appropriate follow-up, and ensure proper stewardship of the gift. Major gift officers are often expert communicators and have good human relations skills. They are senior staff and work closely with administration or management of an organization.

- **Corporate and foundation solicitation:** Seeking funds from these markets involves proposal writing skills, as well as research and team management. Seeking prospects among these two potential funding sources requires the ability to perform research, produce written material, edit copy, bring together persons with different knowledge and expertise, communicate with prospects, provide follow-up information, develop appropriate recognition procedures, and be accountable for the use of grant funds.

- **Planned giving:** This is the fastest-growing area of expertise and requires a great deal of technical knowledge balanced with people skills. Planned giving is a demanding but growing subspecialty, which involves learning about the various instruments for giving, tax structures and their implications, and the benefits to the donor and the beneficiaries. Planned giving professionals often are senior-level employees and work with volunteers and the president or executive director.

- **Data and records management:** This includes tracking information and helping others manage the information. Most organizations maintain computer as well as hard-copy records. A professional must know how to enter the information into the database correctly so that it is useful and can be retrieved for specific purposes. Gift receipting and acknowledgment are often a part of this role. An eye for details and patience in following through are critical for this function.

- **Consulting:** This consists of working independently in advising nonprofit organizations. Consultants may specialize or be generalists. They may work independently or with a firm. They will need a broad base of fundraising knowledge and have the ability to give advice.[7]

The titles that go along with these tasks vary a great deal and may or may not reflect the person's rank and role in the organization. Titles include:

- Vice president for institutional advancement (or just advancement)
- Vice president for development or philanthropy
- Resource development officer
- Director of development
- Major gifts officer
- Annual fund director
- Annual giving director
- Fundraising manager
- Planned giving officer or director
- Grants manager
- Corporate and foundation relations specialist or director
- Fundraising coordinator
- Researcher
- Prospect researcher
- Research assistant
- Database manager
- Records manager

---

[7] Lilya Wagner, *Careers in Fundraising* (Hoboken: John Wiley & Sons, 2002).

- Administrative assistant
- Development manager

Even though we have perceptions and concepts of where each of the above functional and descriptive (by title) roles ranks in an organization, leadership skills are needed for each position and function. A research assistant, for example, may be the lowest paid person on a fundraising team, but that person must know how to acquire and use information, communicate with others, listen, be accurate, inform others, and motivate people. These responsibilities require good leadership, no matter what the individual's stated rank or pay.

> *Give someone a real sense of purpose, the feeling that he or she is working for a valuable, mutually important goal. That's where true motivation comes from — motivation not just to go through the motions of working, motivation to excel.*
>
> —Robert Lee and Sara King[8]

Now let's take a look at the last dimension of the model in Exhibit 6.1. The focus of this book is the dotted line on the model, which shows where we as fundraising professionals use the leadership skills that we have learned, developed, refined, and maximized. This means that we not only perform in a status quo manner, as represented by the intersecting line, but also go beyond the expected and minimal performance. We reach the ideal in performance because we have performed our jobs

---

[8] Dale Carnegie & Associates, *The Leader in You* (New York: Pocket Books, 1993), p. 43. Robert J. Lee, Sara N. King, and the Center for Creative Leadership, *Discovering the Leader in You: A Guide to Realizing Your Personal Leadership Potential* (San Francisco: Jossey-Bass, 2001).

with excellence; motivated and influenced others to take action; encouraged our colleagues, subordinates, superiors, and constituents; served as a symbol by giving and performing well; and practiced the renewal of spirit, process, procedure, and goal.

A perennial favorite of leadership literature is Max De Pree; he presents eight keys to effective nonprofit leadership and how to implement them. These will serve as our benchmarks as we achieve the ideal point in our leadership model and truly can practice leading from the middle.

1. **A sense of stewardship:** Keeping our promises and maintaining public confidence.

2. **A compelling vision:** Articulating the implications of shared values and envisioning possibilities based on convictions.

3. **Affirmation without arrogance:** Having courage and resolve and cultivating commitment without conceit.

4. **Political savvy:** Understanding and performing the process through which things get done and exerting positive influence.

5. **Strategic thinking:** The efficient progress of mission-related measurable objectives and influencing ownership.

6. **Intelligent risk-taking:** Being appropriately entrepreneurial and willing to change.

7. **Concern for quality:** Achieving excellence.

8. **Empowerment:** Understanding that ours is not a solo act but a group performance.[9]

Leadership, De Pree says, is a melodic blend. "A leader sets the example for openness and imagination and acceptance. A leader remains

---

[9] G. Worth George, "Leadership Jazz: Selected Themes for Orchestrating Nonprofit Quality," *Nonprofit World,* vol. 2, issue 2 (March/April 1993), pp. 28–32.

responsible for making the future promising and making promises for the future. A leader who makes no promises leaves a vacuum."[10]

REFLECTIONS

Using the model presented earlier in Exhibit 6.1, jot down your organizational leadership requirements as well as your positional leadership responsibilities. Below is a copy of the model, so that you can actually write on the model itself. Then write down the leadership qualities, tactics, and skills you can use to reach the ideal.

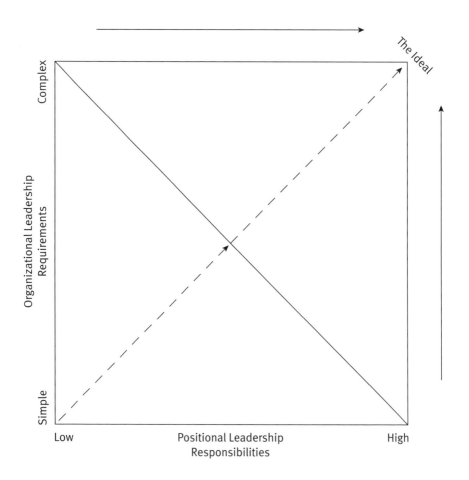

[10] *Ibid.*, p. 32.

DEVELOP YOUR SKILLS

Below is a table listing the qualities that a person can develop for leadership. For each quality, add phrases on how that quality can be developed, then indicate what you will do to develop it.

Leadership Quality	What Can Be Done to Develop It	What You Will Do to Develop It
Energy and perseverence	Seek problems to solve rather than waiting, assert ideas and hold on to them, take care of your personal health	
Education and scholarship	Read, attend conferences and workshops, get training	
Good judgment	Think before you speak, rehearse to attain verbal facility, make reasonable and dependable judgments, set an example	
Self-confidence	Don't think about what you'll do if you don't succeed, think about what you'll do when you make it, set achievable goals	
Creativity, initiative, innovativeness	Maintain an open mind about possibilities, seek new ideas, implement worthwhile ideas	
Enthusiasm and optimism	Have an upbeat demeanor, watch your voice and body language	
Communicating and listening	Polish your writing and speaking skills, remember that people want to be listened to, be alert and keep focused on what the other person is saying	
Devotion to excellence	Aim high but be realistic, be careful in your work, ask for others to check your work, avoid the half-done task, be an example	
Decisive yet fair	Practice making decisions by looking at options and coming up with the best solution for all involved, don't avoid decision making, or delay a decision	

(continues)

(Continued)

Leadership Quality	What Can Be Done to Develop It	What You Will Do to Develop It
High ethical standards	Study the ethical guidelines that leading thinkers have written about, urge your CEO and board to set policies for ethical behavior, know what you believe and why, act according to your beliefs	
Vision	Look ahead, don't get bogged down with everyday duties, look for possibilities instead of problems	
Exhibit constancy and have congruity	It's okay to change your mind, but try to avoid keeping people uncertain by making too many switches of opinion and action, make sure your deeds match your words	
Integrity, possess real convictions	Be honest, maintain your standards and values	

FOR FURTHER READING

Additional readings can be found at the end of the book.

William J. Bennett. *Virtues of Leadership.* Nashville, TN: W Publishing, a division of Thomas Nelson, 2001.

Lee G. Bolman and Terrence E. Deal. *Leading with Soul: An Uncommon Journey of Spirit.* San Francisco: Jossey-Bass, 2001.

Richard L. Daft and Robert H. Lengel. *Fusion Leadership: Unlocking the Subtle Forces That Change People and Organizations.* San Francisco: Berrett-Koehler, 2000.

Max De Pree. *Leadership Jazz.* New York: Dell, 1992.

CHAPTER 7

Servant Leadership for the Fundraiser

Adaptation of Greenleaf's theories and how well they exemplify what fundraisers do and the roles they play.

During America's first war, a corporal asked his men to cut down some trees to make a bridge. The work went slowly because there weren't enough men. Then a man with a commanding presence rode up and spoke to the officer in charge, who was urging the men to work harder but did nothing himself. "You don't have enough men for the job, do you," said the man on horseback.

"No, sir. We need some help."

"Why don't you lend a hand yourself?"

"Me, sir? Why, I'm a corporal," said the officer, rather offended by the suggestion.

"Ah, true," replied the man as he slid off his horse. He worked alongside the men until the job was done, then said as he rode off, "Corporal, the next time you have a job to accomplish and too few men to do it, you should send for the commander in chief, and I will come again." The man on horseback was General Washington.[1]

---

[1] Adapted from William J. Bennett, *Virtues of Leadership* (Nashville, TN: W Publishing, a division of Thomas Nelson, 2001).

The prince is the first servant of his state.

—Frederick the Great[2]

Whether the story is true or apocryphal, like that about George Washington and the cherry tree, it makes a good point and great men and women have often set an example of leadership through service.

More than 2000 years ago, the Chinese philosopher Lao-Tzu wrote, "The leader is one who serves." This ancient wisdom began undergoing a revival by Robert Greenleaf in the 1970s. He had spent most of his professional life in management research, development, and education at AT&T. At age 60, he began a new career and established a small think tank, the Center for Applied Ethics. He got caught up in the spirit of the 1960s, which questioned authority, and began a search for new sources of legitimacy. At the end of that decade, he wrote "The Servant as Leader," an essay he circulated to encourage people to take on more responsibility. He served as consultant to many prestigious organizations and as a lecturer in higher educational institutions such as MIT and Harvard.

He wrote in *Servant Leadership,* "An institution starts on a course toward people-building with leadership that has a firmly established context of people first. With that, the right actions fall naturally into place."[3] Successful leaders, fundraisers included, will be those who are

---

[2] Frederick the Great, *Memoirs of the House of Brandenburg, 1758,* as quoted in John Bartlett, *Bartlett's Familiar Quotations: A Collection of Passages, Phrases, and Proverbs Traced to Their Sources in Ancient and Modern Literature* (Boston: Little, Brown, 2002), p. 330.

[3] Sheila Murray Bethel, *Beyond Management to Leadership: Designing the 21st Century Association* (Washington, DC: The Foundation of the American Society of Association Executives, 1993), p. 6.

willing to serve—not just their superiors, to whom they have an obligation of service, but staff, board, volunteers, colleagues, constituents,
and in particular, donors. Greenleaf's words, written in 1977, apply more
than ever today:

> A new moral principle is emerging which holds that the only
> authority deserving one's allegiance is that which is freely and
> knowingly granted by the led to the leader in response to, and in
> proportion to, the clearly evident servant stature of the leader.
> Those who choose to follow this principle will not casually accept
> the authority of existing institutions. Rather, they will freely
> respond only to individuals who are chosen as leaders because
> they are proven and trusted as servants."[4]

Greenleaf wanted to make sure that others' needs were met. Therefore,
he suggested that leaders must listen, leaders must accept others as peers,
and leaders must have the foresight to move forward (see Exhibit 7.1).

Developing the qualities of servant leadership isn't easy because the
servant leader must be more selfless than selfish. It also requires much
tolerance for imperfection while striving for excellence. The training
of U.S. Marines perhaps has it right. One of the Marines' mottos is,
"Serve your troops first that you may command them better."

C. William Pollard, chairman of The ServiceMaster Company, which
has been recognized by *Fortune* magazine as the number one service
company among the Fortune 500, wrote that servant leadership was a
motto of his company. He believed that the company was successful
because it practiced this type of leadership. First, he said, his company
recognizes the dignity and worth of all people. Second, servant leaders
must be committed. They keep promises, they listen and learn, and
they make things happen. Servant leaders are givers, not takers. They
promote diversity, and they provide an environment where people can

---

[4] *Ibid.,* p. 9.

EXHIBIT 7.1   THE SERVANT LEADER MODEL

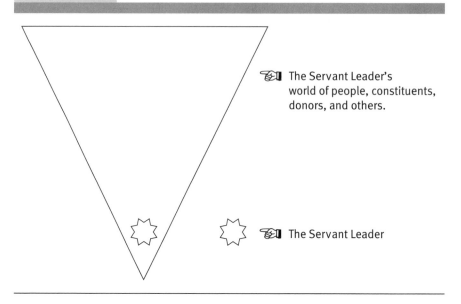

☞ The Servant Leader's world of people, constituents, donors, and others.

☞ The Servant Leader

learn and grow. Servant leaders, Pollard said, must be value driven and performance oriented.[5]

Pollard wrote, "As leaders, we recognize that we are all prisoners of our hope. Our hope sustains us. Our vision of what could be inspires us and those we lead. . . . A servant leader's results will be measured beyond the workplace, and the story will be told in the changed lives of others."[6]

Greenleaf's own writing was quite academic and at times convoluted, but many others have taken his words and put them into a more accessible format. Walter Kiechel, III, writing in *Fortune,* explained what he called "a few of the more beguiling aspects of the servant leader.[7]

[5] Frances Hesselbein, Marshall Goldsmith, and Richard Beckhard (eds.), *The Leader of the Future* (New York: The Drucker Foundation, 1996).

[6] Hesselbein et al., *The Leader of the Future,* p. 248.

[7] Walter Kiechel, III. "The Leader as Servant," *Fortune* (May 4, 1992), p. 122.

The servant leader takes people, and their work, really seriously. Kiechel quotes Greenleaf as saying, "The work exists for the person as much as the person exists for the work."[8]

For the fundraising professional, this holds much truth. We do our work because of our donors and the causes to which they give. And we do the work because of our commitment to the mission and to excellence in service.

The servant leader listens. Building consensus, soliciting everyone's view, and coming to mutually agreeable and workable conclusions requires much listening. The fundraiser must listen to the organization and what its personnel are saying, must listen to what the donor needs and wants to accomplish, and must listen to the broader needs defined by the mission.

The servant leader heals. Servant leadership requires a kind of openness, a willingness to share in mistakes and pain. The fundraiser as servant leader doesn't lay blame but shares it, and much of the work of the fundraiser involves healing pain, making things better for the client, the community, and, thereby, society.

The servant leader is self-effacing. The fundraiser doesn't brag about what he or she did. Because fundraising requires teamwork—the cooperation of the volunteers, the staff, and the organizational leader—the collective praise and success is what motivates further success.

The servant leader sees himself as a steward. The fundraiser ensures that the donors' wishes are honored, that funds are spent as promised, that the donor and the client are both respected as their needs are met, and that the fundraising process is carried out with integrity and attention to ethics.[9]

---

[8] *Ibid.*, p. 122.

[9] Adapted from Kiechel, *The Leader as Servant*, p. 121.

The understanding of the mission and the ability to express it clearly is often the thing that sets a person apart as a leader.

—Robert P. Neuschel[10]

Larry Spears, who directs the Greenleaf Leadership Center, wrote that servant leadership requires these traits:[11]

- Listening

- Empathy

- Healing

- Awareness

- Persuasion

- Conceptualization

- Foresight

- Stewardship

- Commitment to the growth of people

- Building community

Certainly, these are a good summary of what servant leadership is all about. Fundraisers are servant leaders. We build trust, we forge teams, we get things done through others, we communicate, we envision, and

---

[10] Robert P. Neuschel, *The Servant Leader: Unleashing the Power of Your People* (East Lansing: Visions Sports Management Group, 1998), p. 58.

[11] Larry C. Spears and Michele Lawrence, *Focus on Leadership: Servant-Leadership for the Twenty-First Century* (Hoboken: John Wiley & Sons, 2002).

we care. As John Heider stated in *The Tao of Leadership,* "True self-interest teaches selflessness. Heaven and earth endure because they are not simply selfish but exist in behalf of all creation. The wise leader, knowing this, keeps egocentricity in check and by doing so becomes even more effective. Enlightened leadership is service, not selfishness. The leader grows more and lasts longer by placing the well-being of all above the well-being of self alone."[12]

REFLECTIONS

Challenge yourself. Ask yourself these questions.

- As a fundraising professional, how do I assess myself in the servant leader role?

- How can I strengthen that role?

- How effectively am I setting the example of a servant leader?

- What action can I take to inspire others to accept this role as well?

DEVELOP YOUR SKILLS

Evaluate yourself as a servant leader. Using the table on the following page, review your experiences as a servant leader. Can you identify a time when you were particularly good at one of the characteristics enumerated by Greenleaf? What made you successful in "living" this characteristics? In the last column, identify one task you will undertake in order to improve each of the servant leadership qualities.

---

[12] John Heider, *The Tao of Leadership: Lao Tzu's Tao Te Ching Adapted for a New Age* (New York: Bantam Books, 1986), p. 13.

Servant Leader Characteristic	Your Successful Experience in Using This Characteristic	What You Will Do to Improve This Characteristic and Its Use
Listening		
Empathy		
Healing		
Awareness		
Persuasion		
Conceptualization		
Foresight		

Servant Leader Characteristic	Your Successful Experience in Using This Characteristic	What You Will Do to Improve This Characteristic and Its Use
Stewardship		
Commitment to the growth of people		
Building community		

FOR FURTHER READING

Additional readings can be found at the end of the book.

Robert K. Greenleaf. *Servant: Retrospect and Prospect.* Indianapolis, IN: The Robert K. Greenleaf Center, 1990.

Robert K. Greenleaf. *Servant Leadership: A Journey Into the Nature of Legitimate Power and Greatness.* New York: Paulist Press, 1977.

Walter Kiechel, III. "The Leader as Servant," *Fortune* (May 4, 1992).

Robert P. Neuschel. *The Servant Leader: Unleashing the Power of Your People.* East Lansing, MI: Visions Sports Management Group, 1998.

Larry C. Spears and Michele Lawrence. *Focus on Leadership: Servant-Leadership for the Twenty-First Century.* Hoboken: John Wiley & Sons, 2002.

CHAPTER 8

Desirable and Required Leadership Competencies

The sections of this chapter address the salient concepts that fundraisers must have to become leaders—not by position or power but by practices that define true leadership. The sections include:

- *Leading for loyalty*
- *Leading for innovation*
- *Leading to build*
- *Balancing humility and assertiveness*
- *Facilitative leadership*
- *Emotional intelligence*
- *Ethical practice*
- *Diversity and multicultural challenges*
- *Leading from mission*
- *Survival versus vision*

When Vince Lombardi led the Green Bay Packers onto Lambeau Field on December 31, 1967, the team was playing for its third consecutive NFC championship and a shot at winning its second consecutive

Super Bowl. Lombardi and the Packers knew they would be facing a tough opponent in Tom Landry's Dallas Cowboys. But nobody on the field at the beginning of play that day realized he would be playing in one of the most memorable games in the history of the National Football League."[1]

As the story goes, the temperature that day was inhospitable at 13 degrees below zero, but the "ice bowl," as it would later be known, was only a sidebar to a historic game. In the fourth quarter, with only 16 seconds left, the Cowboys were leading 17–14. Coach Lombardi called in the quarterback, Bart Starr, and said, "Run it, and let's get the hell out of here." Starr then crossed the goal line in a daring move, and the Packers went on to Miami, where they won in Super Bowl II.

Lombardi is known more for his philosophy of "Winning isn't everything; it's the only thing," (perhaps an apocryphal statement) than for his leadership style and skills. The myth of Lombardi pictures him as an iron-willed command-and-control manager, but in reality his style was based on the concept of freedom through discipline—"you practice and refine and perfect something so that it becomes second nature to you, and once you have that discipline, you can react more freely when obstacles or troubles arise."[2] Lombardi later admitted that he didn't know what Starr was going to do, but he trusted the quarterback's judgment because it was based on discipline.

When the myths of Lombardi are stripped away, we see a great inspirational leader who stood for passion, integrity, discipline, and a willingness to adapt to changing circumstances. These are the keys to effective leadership.

---

[1] Dayton Fandray, "Lombardi's Lessons," *Continental* (January 2004), p. 27.

[2] *Ibid.,* p. 28.

What do we, or should we, stand for in our leadership practice? The themes and topics can vary greatly in number, but here are those that may be most significant for fundraising professionals to acquire.

First, let's look at *leading for loyalty*. Loyalty of colleagues, subordinates, management, donors, constituents, and any others with whom we come in contact cannot be bought. It must be earned, and the first way to do that is to practice what you preach.[3] Holding the right values isn't enough. We need to clarify and share them with all, and do so in words and deeds. This is a particularly valuable concept for fundraisers, because fundraising is an exchange of values.

Other ways that fundraisers can develop loyalty through leadership is by creating win-win situations for their organizations and their donors. True partnerships serve the interests of both parties. This means careful

---

Where is that chain of command when you need it? If you're like most managers, you regularly find yourself in situations where you have responsibility but not authority to get things done through a group. Maybe you head up a cross-functional team whose members don't report to you. . . . Or maybe you do have nominal authority, but find that your charges — software engineers, hotshot Gen X marketers, whoever — respond to directives the way a cat responds to the command "roll over." In all such cases, issuing direct orders is part of the problem, not part of the solution. As Peter Drucker puts it, "you have to learn to manage in situations where you don't have command authority, where you are neither controlled nor controlling."[4]

---

[3] The principles discussed here are adapted from Frederick F. Reichheld. "Lead for Loyalty," *Harvard Business Review* (July-August 2001), pp. 76–84.

[4] "How to Lead When You're Not the Boss," *Harvard Management Update,* a newsletter from Harvard Business School Publishing, volume 5, number 3 (March 2000).

selection of donors and the case we make to them for funding support. A good experience will mean increased loyalty that can also be maintained. In addition, keep it simple. It's a complex world, and we do our donors a favor if we show accountability and responsibility in simple ways.

Providing rewards for the right results is another principle of loyalty. Recognition that is appropriate for the donor and the gift is appreciated and loyalty is increased. Finally, listen carefully and talk straight. This improves two-way communication that is critical for two-way loyalty. High standards of considerate behavior don't impede progress. Organizations thrive when their employees and external partners thrive. Through loyalty to high ideals, leaders become worthy of loyalty from their partners/donors.

Second, let's look at *leading for innovation*. According to a study by Rosabeth Moss Kanter, those who foster innovative growth-oriented accomplishments share a set of personal qualities—thoroughness, persistence, discretion, persuasiveness, and comfort with change. Innovators generally aren't firebrands or revolutionaries. They work through existing networks to uncover opportunities, build coalitions, and make change happen.[5] Fundraisers must be innovative because of fluctuation in the economy, in the fundraising environment both internally and externally, in the unexpected challenges such as demands for accountability or government oversight. Therefore, they must work confidently with uncertainties and see unmet needs as opportunities. They must choose their projects and goals carefully and with long-term sustainability of the organization as the primary goal. They are required to be thorough and to understand that they cannot achieve their goals overnight, and, therefore, fundraisers must persevere.

---

[5] Rosabeth Moss Kanter. "The Middle Manager as Innovator, *Harvard Business Review* (July-August 2004), pp. 150–161.

Third, let's look at *leading to build*. In the for-profit world, there is often an outcry that we're lacking a new generation of leaders. Those companies that do grow and nurture new leaders are known as leader-builders. In the same way, fundraisers must ensure a legacy of professionals and, therefore, nurture and mentor newer and/or younger generations of fundraisers who can also be leaders. Experts in the area of leader-builders have outlined several common traits that are applicable to how we, as fundraising professionals, build for the future of our profession by ensuring that there will be qualified individuals available to carry on our legacies. Leader-builders have a strong vision of the future. They display remarkably consistent behaviors, regardless of their level in the organization. There is continuous development and replenishment of the leadership talent pool and pipeline. There is a strong emphasis on the identification of specific leadership competencies that support the organization's mission and strategy, and there is strong commitment to continuous organizational renewal.[6] To ensure the continuity of our organizations and the availability of professionals to bring in funds, we must adopt leader-builder behaviors as valid functions of our leadership.

Fourth, let's look at *balancing humility and assertiveness*. No one likes an arrogant braggart. In fact, there is that perverse trait in most of us that likes to see a brash egomaniac brought to his or her knees.

So, how do we remain assertive enough that we are seen and heard, yet humble enough without becoming invisible? According to Joseph L. Badaracco, Jr., modest, subtle yet tenacious actions often have the greatest impact.[7] A lot is at stake for fundraisers; they must be ready to

---

[6] Adapted from Steve Yearout, Gerry Miles, and Richard Koonce, "Wanted: Leader-Builders," *Training & Development* (March 2000).

[7] Joseph L. Badaracco, Jr., *Leading Quietly* (Boston: Harvard Business School Press, 2002).

roll up their sleeves and play to win. They must be confident in their actions. Sometimes, these desirable traits that winners in the fundraising field have acquired also border on or lead to arrogance. We must then be reminded of why we do what we do—fundraising is for the benefit of the organization and its clients, not for our own benefit. If we remember that we work for a mission and to fulfill human needs, we will keep focused on our true calling. We can be proud of our achievements—and we should be. Fundraising should be done with pride, not apology. But we must never lose sight of the fact that, even when we manage and achieve win-win situation for all, we are the intermediaries, the facilitators of a relationship that results in a winning cause, and it's not about us—it's about others.

Fifth, let's look at *facilitative* leadership. "Leaders often help create the consequences they try to avoid. They seek high-quality decisions but find out that information was not shared with them. They seek commitment from others but get compliance or resistance. They ask the people who report to them to be accountable and take initiative but find themselves having to resolve their staffs' problems. In each of those examples, leaders unknowingly contribute to the consequences they complain about."[8] If you question people's motives when they hold views that differ from yours, if you express negative emotions, act as if your reasoning is foolproof, and keep your strategy to yourself, you cause others to become defensive, and the level of trust falls.

By contrast, a facilitative leader does just the opposite. Such a leader believes in free and informed choice, and aids people in making the right choices because they have information, not because they are manipulated or coerced into a decision. The result then is commitment; people do what is necessary to implement the decision because they

---

[8] Roger Schwarz, "Becoming a Facilitative Leader," *Training and Development* (April 2003), p. 52.

believe it's the right one. A facilitative leader believes in core values and suspends judgments so that other viewpoints can be heard. There is empathy for others, as well as accountability for one's actions. "Becoming a facilitative leader means changing how you think in order to change the consequences you help create."[9]

Fundraising professionals function best when using facilitative leadership skills. They listen to and respect the views of their donors, identify with donors' needs, and are accountable for their actions. Fundraisers facilitate the relationship between donor and organization without implanting their own egos into the relationship the organization has with the donor.

> Abraham Lincoln said "I have an irrepressible desire to live till I can be assured that the world is a little better for my having lived in it."
>
> —Gene Griessman[10]

Sixth, let's look at *emotional intelligence* in leadership. Daniel Goleman is credited with bringing the term to public attention. He maintained that, while necessary, traditional qualities associated with leadership, such as determination, intelligence, and vision, weren't enough. He maintained that effective leaders must have a high degree of emotional intelligence, which included self-awareness, self-regulation, motivation, empathy, and social skill.[11] Some of these topics are addressed in various places in this book, but let's take a look at the overall quality of what it means to have emotional intelligence.

---

[9] *Ibid.*, p. 56.

[10] Gene Griessman, *The Words Lincoln Lived By* (New York: Simon & Schuster, 1997).

[11] Daniel Goleman, "What Makes a Leader?" *Harvard Business Review* (January 2004), pp. 82–91.

Goleman maintains that the five components of emotional skill at work complement intelligence and technical skill and that the addition of emotional intelligence leads to effective performance.

First, we should have the ability to recognize and understand our own moods and emotions, and how these affect others. This realistic self-assessment allows us to move toward self-regulation, the second component. We have the ability to control or reflect on our moods and attitudes, and we think before we act. This component fosters an openness to change and a comfort with ambiguity. We are then motivated to work for reasons that go beyond money or status, and we pursue goals with energy and persistence. We can have optimism even in the face of failure. Moving from motivation, we acquire empathy, the ability to understand the makeup of others' emotions, and become skillful in treating people according to their reactions. This includes cross-cultural sensitivity and expertise in human relations and communication. Finally, we become socially skilled, proficient in managing relationships and building networks through an ability to find common ground and build rapport. This makes us most effective in persuasiveness, building teams, and leading change.[12]

"It was once thought that the components of emotional intelligence were 'nice to have' in business leaders. But now we know that, for the sake of performance, these are ingredients that leaders 'need to have.'"[13]

Seventh, let's look at *ethical practice*. Max De Pree asks, "Where do ethics and leadership intersect?" and then goes on to answer his own question, "Believe me, they do intersect, all the time."[14] Violations of ethics by major corporations in the early twenty-first century brought much attention to the ethical beliefs of a leader and his or her commitment to the organization.

---

[12] *Ibid.*, p. 88.

[13] *Ibid.*, p. 91.

[14] Max De Pree, *Leadership Jazz* (New York: Dell, 1992).

For the fundraiser, ethical practice is of paramount importance. We must gain and keep the trust of our donors through careful stewardship of our relationship with them and stewardship of their funds. Leadership and ethics intersect in the common good. We put the needs of our constituents and donors first, and we need to live exemplary lives and never be at odds with integrity and honesty. Accountability and transparency also contribute to ethical practice. "A leader's commitments and beliefs are part and parcel of the same thing," De Pree concluded. "A true leader cannot commit herself without beliefs."[15]

There are excellent volumes that will help the fundraising leader think through ethical implications, quandaries, and dilemmas and shape their practice and organizations in ethically responsive ways. One of the best of these is by Marilyn Fischer.[16]

Eighth, let's look at *diversity and multicultural challenges.* An immediate caveat is necessary here. These topics merit entire volumes of their own, and many have been written. We include this section as a reminder that leadership is multidimensional, and these dimensions include all the differences we find in gender, culture, ethnicity, and multinationalism.

In *Women of Influence, Women of Vision: A Cross-Generational Study of Leaders and Social Change,* a volume reporting on a study of women and leadership, Helen Astin and Carole Leland state, "In the last two decades the study of women has produced an impressive body of new knowledge and has contributed to the development of new paradigms on leadership."[17] This lengthy study represented a break from traditional models and studies, and redefined who is a leader beyond

---

[15] *Ibid.,* 1992, p. 139.

[16] Marilyn Fischer, *Ethical Decision Making in Fund Raising* (Hoboken: John Wiley and Sons, 2000).

[17] Helen Astin and Carole Leland, *Women of Influence, Women of Vision: A Cross-Generational Study of Leaders and Social Change* (San Francisco: Jossey-Bass, 1991), p. 2.

her position. It laid the groundwork for increasing attention to be placed on the uniqueness that women can bring to leadership.

Building on these types of foundations, Lynne Joy McFarland, Larry E. Senn, and John R. Childress, who compiled *21st Century Leadership: Dialogues with 100 Top Leaders,* included an entire section on Women in Leadership: Embracing Diversity. They state, "Women and diverse ethnic people are crucial to the new leadership currency, which holds no prejudices on gender, race, or creed. The top leaders we interviewed clearly indicate that now is the time to avail ourselves of the unique contributions of women and diverse people — to bring them into greater positions of authority and to effectively empower and educate them to take leadership roles."[18]

A balance of feminine and masculine traits is receiving increased attention, and wise leaders integrate both. Traditionally, the masculine paradigm meant the drive to implement goals and bring about tangible results. Now, the feminine impulse connects diverse opinions and elements and forms them into a whole. "To be successful in the coming years, leaders of organizations and nations will need to embrace the balance of trust and strength, caring and success, process and results."[19]

In addition to these perspectives, there is an increasing global consciousness in all sectors and societies of the world, resulting in increasing diversity in our daily lives. "Leadership practices that recognize diversity as a positive asset of organizations and communities will need to be employed. New systems thinking will be required to design processes that increase inclusiveness and diversity in decision making."[20]

---

[18] Lynne Joy McFarland, Larry E. Senn, and John R. Childress, *21st Century Leadership: Dialogues with 100 Top Leaders* (New York: The Leadership Press, 1993), p. 225.

[19] *Ibid.,* p. 226.

[20] Kellogg Leadership Studies Project, 1994–1997. *Rethinking Leadership* (College Park, MD: The Burns Academy of Leadership Press, 1998), p. 42.

In short, everyone counts. We can't afford to overlook talent, including that possessed by women and diverse populations. We need to build organizations that honor every individual.

Ninth, let's look at *leading from mission*. The substance of any leader's job must be grounded in the deep understanding of the organization's mission. It can't be just lip service or a recitation of nice sounding words. "The effective manager/leader must understand the mission, even help shape it, articulate it convincingly and inspiringly, identify the ongoing tasks important to achieving the mission, and discipline the organization to always concentrate on those tasks that contribute to progress toward the mission."[21] For the fundraiser, an understanding of, adherence to, and commitment to the organization's mission are essential fundamentals for successful fundraising. The development of a case for support is based on the mission, appeals to donors are founded on the mission, and the practice of fundraising should be based on a dedication to the mission as well as a personal mission of excellence in fundraising as a profession.

When writing about organizational alignment and focus, author John Gehrke stated that there are four essential elements in every non-profit organization, and the first of these is mission and vision. Gehrke believes that there are internal and external perspectives of each element. "Vertical alignment describes the staff's understanding of the organization's mission/vision. This alignment is attained when all staff members understand their individual role in the pursuit of the organization's mission. . . . Horizontal alignment references the organization's strategies that are used to serve others." This is a good illustration of the need to reflect, both in a personal mission as well as the overall

---

[21] Robert P. Neuschel, *The Servant Leader: Unleashing the Power of Your People* (East Lansing, MI: Visions Sports Management Group, 1998), p. 84.

mission of the institution because that is what drives our willingness to serve and succeed.[22]

Commitment to a personal mission that is congruent with the organization's mission is fundamental to fundraising. This commitment, followed by actions that support public good and moral purpose, allow donors to trust us and our organizations.

Tenth, let's conclude with a look at *survival versus vision*. We live in turbulent times. Everything in our world is changing fast and not always in expected ways. The fundraiser is often charged with ensuring the organization's survival, and as a consequence, does things the way that has always worked. This may produce sustainability, but also a status quo. Excitement may be lacking, and the organization becomes stagnant.

However, as Jonathan Swift said, "Vision is the art of seeing things invisible."[23] The fundraising leader, while ensuring the survival of the organization, also looks ahead to what can be, and adds another layer to his work—that of accomplishing tasks now that will lead to fruition tomorrow. This is best exemplified by an emphasis on major donor development, a process that can take many months and even years, yet the support of major donors allows for visions to become reality and for the organization to grow.

The words of Warren Bennis, who provided a fine perspective on leading up, best summarize these ideas. "Today's leaders must have more than just absolute power to win respect and followers. . . . They must be willing to inspire a more collaborative approach that lets them tap

---

[22] John Gehrke, "Organizational Alignment and Focus," *Advancing Philanthropy*, Spring 1998, p. 39.

[23] Jonathan Swift, *Thoughts on Various Subjects; on Miscellanies* (1711), from Jonathan Swift, *The Works of Dean Swift: Comprising A Tale of a Tub, The Battle of the Books, with Thoughts and Essays on Various Subjects, Together with The Dean's Advice to a Young Lady on Her Marriage* (New York: Derby & Jackson, 1857).

into the endless source of ideas, innovation, know-how and knowledge of the people they lead."[24]

Believe you me, having to smile and be jolly every day when you're wearing the same thick, hot, red-wool suit (that itches like crazy) is no picnic. This is a job that will definitely strain your sanity and drain your ego if you let it. Seems like everyone wants a piece of me. Yet many of the people I serve question my existence . . . or just plain don't believe in me at all. And those who do believe often expect me to do the impossible—rarely caring about what I have to do, or go through (including chimneys), to meet their expectations. And they ALL have expectations. . . . There's no doubt that my biggest challenges come from two roles that people rarely associate with this red-cheeked, bag-carrying sleigh driver: Santa the MANAGER and Santa the LEADER. So here is a summary of my leadership secrets [at least some of them].

- *Build a wonderful workshop—make the mission the main thing and let values be your guide.*

- *Choose your reindeer wisely—hire tough so you can manage easy, promote the right ones for the right reasons, and go for the diversity advantage.*

- *Make a list and check it twice—plan your work and work your plan.*

- *Listen to the elves—open your ears to participation, pay attention, walk a while in THEIR shoes.*

- *Get beyond the red wagons—help everyone accept the reality of change.*

(continues)

---

[24] Warren Bennis, Ph.D. "Lessons in Leadership from Superconsultant Warren Bennis," *Bottom Line Personal* (July 1, 1996), p. 13.

(Continued)

- *Share the milk and cookies — do right by those who do right.*
- *Be good for goodness sake — set the example and remember that everything counts!*

— Eric Harvey, David Cottrell, and Al Lucia[25]

REFLECTIONS

Take a moment to reflect about your personal mission and vision as a fundraising professional.

- What are you passionate about?
- What are your dreams?
- Where do you want to be in five years? Ten years?
- If you live your life to its fullest, what will you have accomplished?
- What impact do you want to make?[26]

DEVELOP YOUR SKILLS

Discard an assumption. Columbus challenged the Spanish courtiers to stand an egg on its end. They tried but failed. He then hard-boiled one and squashed it down. "That's not fair," they protested, "you broke the

---

[25] Eric Harvey, David Cottrell, and Al Lucia. *The Leadership Secrets of Santa Claus* (Dallas, TX: The Walk the Talk Company, 2003).

[26] The questions are from Robert J. Lee and Sara N. King and the Center for Creative Leadership, *Discovering the Leader in You: A Guide to Realizing Your Personal Leadership Potential* (San Francisco: Jossey-Bass, 2001), p. 33.

rules." "Don't be silly," he replied, "you just assumed more than you needed to."[27]

- What assumptions do you hold about the leadership position and potential of fundraisers?

- What assumptions should you modify?

- Which ones should you eliminate?

- Can you think of an example when you read too much into a situation, and it turned out to be simpler than you thought?

- Mark Twain said, "Habit is habit, and not to be flung out of the window by any man, but coaxed downstairs a step at a time."[28] What leadership habits (name two) do you want to cultivate in yourself?

- What habit do you want to break or minimize that you believe keeps you from practicing good leadership?

FOR FURTHER READING

Additional readings can be found at the end of the book.

While each of the topics discussed in this chapter merit considerable more reading and thought, we believe two are of most importance for the fundraising leader to pursue in more details — fundraising and philanthropy among diverse populations, and ethics and fundraising. Readings for these topics are included below, with annotations, to facilitate your selection of reading.

---

[27] Roger Von Oech, *Creative Whack Pack* (Stamford: U.S. Games Systems, 1992). For more information, go to *www.creativethink.com*.

[28] Mark Twain, *Pudd'nhead Wilson: A Tale* (London: Chatto & Windus, 1894), Chapter 6.

Fundraising and Philanthropy among Diverse Populations

A Special Report—Cultures of Caring: Philanthropy in Diverse American Communities. Washington, DC: Council on Foundations, 1999.

This report examines potential ways to expand the use of institutional philanthropy in four population groups: African Americans, Asian Americans, Latinos and Native Americans.

Patricia O. Bjorhovde, ed. *New Directions for Philanthropic Fundraising,* volume 36, "Creating Tomorrow's Philanthropist: Curriculum Development for Youth," San Francisco: Jossey-Bass, 2002.

This issue examines one specific aspect of youth in philanthropy— the teaching of philanthropy to youth and the curricula being written to accomplish that goal.

Diana Campoamor, W. A. Diaz, and H. A. J. Ramos, eds. *Nuevos Senderos: Reflections on Hispanics & Philanthropy.* Houston: University of Houston, Arte Publico Press, 1999.

These essays provide historical studies, sociological surveys, and analyses of policies and practices in the philanthropic sector.

Julie C. Conry, ed. *New Directions for Philanthropic Fundraising,* volume 19, "Women as Fundraisers," San Francisco: Jossey-Bass, Inc., 1998.

The authors address the opportunities and challenges created by the dramatic increase in the numbers of women pursuing fundraising careers. They highlight the significant ways in which the nonprofit sector is being shaped by women's leadership, and their greater participation in the professional ranks, and many more aspects of women's presence in the field.

Robert E. Fogal, ed. *New Directions for Philanthropic Fundraising,* volume 37, "Fundraising in Diverse Cultural and Giving Environments," San Francisco: Jossey-Bass, 2003.

Some of the topics discussed in this issue are diverse traditions in this country; how African Americans, American Indians, and immigrant families practice philanthropy; and gender differences in the practice of philanthropy. Government funding for faith-based philanthropy is another covered topic.

Marybeth Gasman and Sibby Amderson-Thompkins. *Fund Raising from Black-College Alumni: Successful Strategies for Supporting Alma Mater.* Washington, DC: Council for the Advancement and Support of Education, 2003.

Although black colleges play an important role in the education of Black students, they represent only 3 percent of U.S. institutions of higher education and account for approximately 30 percent of African Americans who receive a bachelor's degree. Alumni giving rates at mostly white institutions of higher education give from 2 percent to 60 percent, while Black college alumni giving falls below 10 percent. This book addresses the causes and makes suggestions for turning this figure around.

Cheryl Hall-Russell and R. H. Kasberg. *African American Traditions of Giving and Serving: A Midwest Perspective.* Indianapolis: The Center on Philanthropy at Indiana University, 1997.

This book details the common patterns of the philanthropic tradition that permeated the laughter and tears of 180 reflective conversations with African Americans in the Midwest.

Charles Hamilton, Warren R. Ilchman, eds. *New Directions for Philanthropic Fundraising,* volume 8, "Cultures of Giving: How Heritage, Gender, Wealth, and Values Influence Philanthropy," San Francisco: Jossey-Bass, 1999.

This is the second of two issues in which the contributors examine how ethnic heritage, gender, wealth, and values influence charitable behavior.

Diana S. Newman. *Opening Doors: Pathways to Diverse Donors.* San Francisco: Jossey-Bass, 2002.

Newman provides insight into the cultural and charitable practices of the African American, Asian American, Latino, and Native American communities. Her book was sponsored by the Council on Foundations and presents a guide not only to help fundraisers understand and reach new donors but also to help them improve the diversity of their development program.

Janice Gow Pettey. *Cultivating Diversity in Fundraising: The AFP/Wiley Fund Development Series.* San Francisco: Jossey-Bass, 2001.

To be successful, fundraisers in today's multicultural world must gain a better understanding of the critical factors that motivate different ethnic groups to give. Written as a guide for those planning to raise funds in diverse communities, the book provides readers with an in-depth understanding of the philanthropic motivation of each of the four major racial/ethic populations.

Janice Gow Pettey, ed. *New Directions for Philanthropic Fundraising,* volume 34, "Diversity in the Fundraising Profession," San Francisco: Jossey-Bass, 2001.

The authors reflect on either distinctions of diversity from within the profession or observations on strategies to enhance diversity in the nonprofit sector.

Sondra C. Shaw and Martha A. Taylor. *Reinventing Fundraising: Realizing the Potential of Women's Philanthropy.* San Francisco: Jossey-Bass, 1995.

This book reveals the reasons why women have not been taken seriously as philanthropists, identifies model programs focusing on women's giving, and outlines new program models that organizations can tailor to their own female constituents.

Bradford S. Smith, Sylvia Shue, J. L. Vest, and J. Villarreal. *Philanthropy in Communities of Color.* Bloomington, IN: Indiana University Press, 1999.

This book describes the specific practices and customs of giving money, goods, and services within communities of color.

Bill Stanczykiewicz, ed. *New Directions for Philanthropic Fundraising,* volume 38, "Engaging Youth in Philanthropy," San Francisco: Jossey-Bass, 2003.

This issue draws from papers delivered August 2002 at the Taking Fundraising Seriously: Youth and Philanthropy symposium sponsored the Center on Philanthropy. How to, legal issues involving youth and philanthropy, and outcomes of engaging and educating youth in philanthropy are discussed in this issue.

Lilya Wagner and Allan Figueroa Deck, eds. *New Directions for Philanthropic Fundraising,* volume 24, "Hispanic Philanthropy." San Francisco: Jossey-Bass, 1999.

The authors explore the factors that influence giving and asking in the Hispanic community. They report on research conducted with leading Hispanic philanthropists, fundraising professionals, and nonprofit executives about the current status of giving and asking in Hispanic American communities and their attitudes and beliefs about philanthropy.

Ronald Austin Wells. *The Honor of Giving: Philanthropy in Native America.* Indianapolis: The Center on Philanthropy at Indiana University, 1998.

This report explores the ways, means, and meanings of philanthropic giving, receiving, obligation, reciprocity, exchange and community across more than a dozen indigenous cultures native to North America.

Ethics and Fundraising

Albert Anderson. *Ethics for Fundraisers.* Bloomington, IN: Indiana University Press, 1996.

This book provides good insight into the relationship between ethics and fundraising.

Alan R. Andreasen, ed. *Ethics in Social Marketing.* Washington, DC: Georgetown University Press, 2001.

Several objectives are covered in this book, presented in a series of papers. These objectives include presenting some of the major ethical problems that social marketers face, offering the reader a sense of the complexity of the ethical dilemmas that social marketers face, providing a framework within which individuals and organizations can make ethical decisions, and trying to increase the likelihood that social marketers will pay increasing attention to maintaining high ethical standards.

Marriane G. Briscoe, ed. *New Directions for Philanthropic Fundraising,* volume. 6, "Ethics in Fundraising: Putting Values into Practice." San Francisco: Jossey-Bass, Inc., 1994.

This groundbreaking sourcebook takes a major step toward developing a code of professional ethics for fundraisers. The examination of the fundraising profession in the moral life of a civil society is the topic of the first three chapters. These chapters are meant to give fundraisers a better and more elevated view of their work as much as to help their donors, bosses, and friends understand that fundraising may be difficult work, but it is certainly not dirty work.

Daniel Conway and Cecelia Hart Price, eds. *New Directions for Philanthropic Fundraising,* volume 17, "The Practice of Stewardship in Religious Fundraising," San Francisco: Jossey-Bass, 1997.

In this issue the authors discuss the accountability of the fundraiser to the donor and public. Includes an interview with Henry Rosso, a leader in professionalization of fundraising.

The Committee on Values and Ethics. *Ethics and the Nation's Voluntary and Philanthropic Community.* Washington, DC: Independent Sector, 1991.

A resource that brings together the standards and statements on ethics adopted by many of the leading philanthropic organizations of America.

This is a valuable resource for developing or revising a nonprofit's own policies.

Marilyn Fischer. *Ethical Decision Making in Fund Raising.* Hoboken: John Wiley & Sons, 2000.

This insightful book presents an ethical decision making model, which will aid fundraisers and other leaders in nonprofit organizations to approach complex situations in a carefully structured manner.

Michael O'Neill, ed. *Ethics in Nonprofit Management.* San Francisco: Institute for Nonprofit Organization Management, 1990.

A collection of cases developed by nonprofit practitioners, scholars, and ethicists that can be used to stimulate moral reasoning and discussion.

PART THREE

Transforming Yourself: Meeting the Challenge of Leading Up

CHAPTER 9

Do You Have the Will to Lead?

Understanding your motivations to provide leadership,
the personal joys and sacrifices necessary to exert leadership,
pitfalls of leadership and how to avoid them.

A 55-year-old fundraising executive is thinking about his next job. He doesn't want to leave his position, but he's stuck where he is. He's not sure he has the energy to search for a better position, but he feels like he's a loser if he doesn't. Maybe I should consider early retirement, he thinks.

The president of a hospital foundation discovers that glitches in the institutional plan will also delay the public announcement of the capital campaign she's been working on. Donors are eager to know what the progress is, but she can't publicize who the lead funders are without knowing how the institution's plan will get back on track. She ponders what kind of success she can predict for herself and the campaign and, more importantly, if she has the gumption, will, and opportunity to be part of the overall solution so that success can be relished by everyone.

A fast-track fundraising professional just five years out of college wants the lifestyle of a well-paid manager, but also feels the need to have a home life and social engagement. How can I make all this happen?

he asks himself. Are my goals so unreasonable, or do I have to refine them? Is a power position really for me?

Pursuing success in fundraising can be like shooting at a series of moving targets at a state fair. Many challenges crop up; as soon as we've achieved one goal, several others pop up. We feel the pressure to work harder, earn more, raise more money, exert more effort, get more publicity and recognition.

What are some of the assumptions about our leadership roles as fundraisers? Perhaps it's a pathway to enduring success—getting what we want with rewards that are meaningful to us and those whom we care about. Perhaps it's attaining something legitimate and important. Or maybe adopting leadership roles delivers a satisfaction that is beyond a momentary reward and is lasting.

Understanding what we want comes before our ability to define and implement how, when, and why we want to develop leadership traits and habits. This means that we have to have change power, first for ourselves and then for others. Whatever role you plan to perform in the organization and the fundraising program, you are an active participant in the changes around you. You can choose your attitude about what's happening, and you can choose your actions. Pat McLagan, writing in "Claim your Change Power," says, "In many people's change lexicon, change participants are divided into the thinkers and the doers. The thinkers (leaders) plan the changes. The doers (followers) implement them, with minimum questioning and challenge. It's true that formal leaders are responsible for creating direction and providing resources for major change initiatives. But followers are *not* passive recipients and order takers. In today's complex world, the members of any community both think and do. Followers (and everyone is a follower in some way) play at least three important, active, and conscious roles."[1] McLagan goes

---

[1] Pat McLagan, "Claim Your Change Power," *Training & Development* (October 2001), p. 60.

on to explain that the first role in effecting change is to be an innovator, one who sees new challenges and offers suggestions for early opportunities for change. The second role is as self-manager, one who tries to understand what really is going on, what he or she will have to do, what values or beliefs to examine, what stand to take, and how to participate for mutual benefit—the organization's and his or her own. The third role is to be a risk taker, a role that may bring some discomfort on both a personal and organizational level. A stand may need to be taken for making changes and letting go of assumptions, fears, and biases while moving out of one's comfort zone may be necessary although threatening as well.

> *Few will have the greatness to bend history; but each of us can work to change a small portion of events, and in the total of all those acts will be written the history of this generation. . . . It is from numberless diverse acts of courage and belief that human history is thus shaped. Each time a man [or woman] stands up for an ideal, or acts to improve the lot of others, or strikes out against injustice, he [or she] sends forth a tiny ripple of hope, and crossing each other from a million different centers of energy and daring, those ripples build a current which can sweep down the mightiest walls of oppression and resistance.*
>
> —Robert Kennedy, Day of Affirmation Address,
> University of Capetown, South Africa, June 6, 1966

First, consider what leadership qualities you want to cultivate in yourself. Throughout this book, leadership traits and behaviors are presented, and in the last chapter you were asked to begin considering change. In the next chapter, we will discuss how to effect change. At the moment, however, consider the change process and how you can define what you wish to change and why.

In an article titled "Transforming Your Leadership Style," John Schuster presents two categories of leadership style—transactional and transformational. Transactional represents some of our old assumptions about leadership—powerbrokering, withholding favors, and quid pro quo. It's best for networking and worst when abusing power. Positional power, status, and influence are paramount in this category.

Better is transformational leadership, which appeals to people's higher levels of motivation to contribute to a cause, and it does not depend on position. While transformational leadership may use some transactional strategies, such as networking, affirming, and doing favors, it does not resort to fear, bribes, or flattery. Perhaps both categories can be seen as on a continuum, as we favor the high end of transformational leadership.[2]

Schuster describes transformational capacities that a person learning to lead might consider. These are adapted below for the fundraising professional.

- **Holding a vision that is intellectually rich, stimulating and true:** You want your life to stand for something, and you do this by transforming the organization and its services through providing funds for accomplishing this vision. You also will develop a vision for your own life and evaluate whether or not it matches the organization's vision.

- **Being honest and empathetic:** People will know you have their interests at heart when you ask them for money. Your credibility grows as you put others before yourself.

- **Developing character, without ego:** Your colleagues and constituents will trust you because your behavior aligns with your words.

---

[2] Adapted from John P. Schuster, "Transforming Your Leadership Style," *Leadership* (1994), pp. 39–40.

- **Expressing a concern for the whole:** Your allegiance to the organization and its donors encompasses your profession.

- **Developing others:** You mentor, you support your appointed leaders, and you build a team for fundraising as you also provide professional opportunities for those who look to you for leadership. You also help donors find fulfillment by giving and volunteering.

- **Sharing power:** You believe this is the best way to engage others and get the work done. You know that teamwork is vital to fundraising, and you understand that power comes in many forms available to you—information sharing, influencing, and motivating others, for starters.

- **Experimenting and taking risks:** Information is never complete, and fundraising responsibilities are never accomplished to a final end because fundraising is an ongoing process, so you continue moving yourself and your donors toward that common vision while trying new ways of doing things that may surpass the success of the old.

- **Being passionate about work:** You commit the right amount of time, attention to detail, and energy to accomplishing your work. Your donors can see that you care about what you do and will be inclined to help you for the sake of the cause.

- **Communicating effectively:** You write, speak, and listen well—with all constituents, from the boss to the donor.

- **Understanding management and administration:** You realize that you're part of the organizational process, and you manage yourself, your tasks, your paperwork, your relationships, while you also respect and follow administration's lead.

- **Celebrating the "now" while looking ahead to the future:** You provide recognition, you celebrate achievements, and you bring an energy and enthusiasm to the organization.

- **Persisting in hard times:** You have the courage to move ahead even when crises occur, you're tired, or you're getting mixed signals, and even when your efforts seem to be thwarted at every turn.[3]

Making the changes you have decided are necessary in order to develop and provide leadership in your fundraising program takes two capacities—the intellectual (the head) and the emotional (the heart). You can think about why you wish to be a leader at whatever level or rank you serve, and you can analyze and plan how to effect change. On the other hand, you also realize that the feelings, emotions, reactions you have to your work are significant and can influence the change you wish to make—justifiably so. Depending on personality type, either of these capacities may dominate, but a balance between these is most desirable. It might be good to remember, as you perform the analysis for deciding on your will to lead, the advice by Edgar Schein in *Leader of the Future*. He says, "Leaders of the future will, therefore, have to have more of the following characteristics," and he lists six qualities for which we can strive as we develop both our will to lead and our capacity to do so:

1. Extraordinary levels of perception and insight.

2. Extraordinary levels of motivation to go through the pain of learning and change.

3. Emotional strength to manage anxiety, your own and that of others, as learning and change become more of a way of life.

4. New skills in analyzing assumptions and evolving processes.

5. Willingness and ability to involve others and get their participation.

---

[3] The qualities presented in John P. Schuster, "Transforming Your Leadership Style," *Leadership* (1994) were adapted for fundraising leadership.

6. Willingness and ability to share power and control according to people's knowledge and skill.[4]

What is the "glue" that holds organizations together? Here is what a recipe might look like.

Fill the glue with fresh, pure, clear water of undiluted human spirit.

Take special care not to contaminate with preconceived ideas, or to pollute with excess control.

Fill slow; notice that the pot only fills from the bottom up. It's impossible to fill it from the top down!

Stir in equal parts of customer focus and pride in good work.

Bring to a boil and blend in a liberal portion of diversity, one part self-esteem, and one part tolerance.

Fold in accountability.

Simmer until smooth and thick, stirring with shared leadership and clear goals.

Season with a dash of humor and a pinch of adventure.

Let cool, then garnish with a topping of core values.

This is only one recipe. Each organization [and fundraiser] must come up with its own. And it must do its own cooking. The new glue cannot be bought off the shelf.

—Richard M. Noer[5]

---

[4] Edgar H. Schein, "Leadership and Organizational Culture" in Frances Hesselbein, Marshall Goldsmith, Richard Beckhard (eds.), *The Leader of the Future* (New York: The Drucker Foundation, 1996), pp. 67–68.

[5] Richard M. Noer, "A Recipe for Glue" in Frances Hesselbein, Marshall Goldsmith, and Richard Beckhard (eds.), *The Leader of the Future* (New York: The Drucker Foundation, 1996), pp. 144–145.

As Richard Beckhard wrote in *The Leader of the Future,* "Truly effective leaders in the years ahead will have personas determined by strong values and belief in the capacity of individuals to grow. They will have an image of the society in which they would like their organizations and themselves to live. They will be visionary, they will believe strongly that they can and should be shaping the future, and they will act on those beliefs through their personal behavior."[6] Fundraisers are some of the best in determining the vision for how their organizations will be in the society all desire and, therefore, must exert leadership in helping others catch this vision as well.

Warren Bennis, well-known for decades as a thought leader in the leadership field, suggested the following for how to become an outstanding leader:

- Be your own teacher—take charge.

- Don't stand on the sidelines—get involved, get new ideas, get challenging assignments.

- Practice your skills as often as possible.

- Reflect on your experience.

- Assume responsibility for your failures.[7]

Before closing this chapter on "the will to lead" and how to change and take charge as you develop your appropriate leadership style for fundraising, let's look at the pitfalls of leadership. A book well worth

---

[6] Richard Beckhard, "On Future Leaders" in Frances Hesselbein, Marshall Goldsmith, and Richard Beckhard (ed.), *The Leader of the Future* (New York: The Drucker Foundation, 1996), p. 129.

[7] Warren Bennis, Ph.D., "Lessons in Leadership from Superconsultant Warren Bennis," *Bottom Line Personal* (July 1, 1996), pp. 13–14.

reading is *The Top Ten Mistakes Leaders Make,* by Hans Finzel.[8] While it's an easy read, this book has a thoughtful perspective of what leadership is and its pitfalls. Finzel lists 10 mistakes, and each can be well applied to the fundraising professional/leader:

1. **The top-down attitude:** This is the number one leadership hang-up. Either fundraisers don't take appropriate leadership responsibility, which they abdicate to assigned leaders, or they resent such leadership.

2. **Putting paperwork before peoplework:** Fundraisers might get caught up in the process rather than the end result, which involves human relationships.

3. **Absence of affirmation:** Fundraisers may forget to say "thanks," internally or externally, and thank others at all levels of the organizations who have helped achieve goals.

4. **No room for mavericks:** Fundraisers may get stuck in the nitty-gritty of daily assignments and fail to look to the future.

5. **Dictatorship in decision-making:** A mindset of "I know all the answers" will certainly get a fundraiser into trouble.

6. **Dirty delegation:** Goal-driven and success motivated fundraisers could refuse to relax, let go, and help others do it.

7. **Communication chaos:** Fundraisers may give mixed signals, forget to communicate, see information as power and not share it, or communicate inappropriately.

8. **Missing the clues of corporate culture:** Often the unseen killer of many a leader, corporate culture will closely affect how

---

[8] Hans Finzel, *The Top Ten Mistakes Leaders Make* (Colorado Springs: Cook Communications, 2000).

fundraising is perceived and accomplished. Awareness of this is key to fundraising success, and working to change corporate culture, while difficult, can begin with fundraising.

9. **Success without successors:** Fundraisers may forget to mentor, to inform board and volunteers about donors and fundraising, and, therefore, cause chaos when they take other jobs.

10. **Failure to focus on the future:** While the present needs are vital and pressing, fundraisers may stay in that stance and forget that donors and the organization need vision, and leadership to move toward that vision.[9]

> *You do not lead by hitting people over the head — that is assault, not leadership.*
>
> —Dwight D. Eisenhower[10]

A compilation of information — the conventional wisdom of leadership failures — includes the following additional traits. While many of these are well known, a short reminder of what can bring us down may be worthwhile. So, what can derail a leader? Personal characteristics and external circumstances that may be termed as "fatal flaws," such as:

- **Insensitivity to others; abrasive, intimidating, bullying style:** "He wouldn't negotiate." "He wouldn't take other people's views." "He wasn't sensitive to the needs of other employees or to our donor market segments."

---

[9] Adapted from Hans Finzel, *The Top Ten Mistakes Leaders Make* (Colorado Springs: Cook Communications, 2000).

[10] Dwight D. Eisenhower quoted in Hans Finzel, *The Top Ten Mistakes Leaders Make* (Colorado Springs: Cook Communications, 2000).

- **Coldness, aloofness, arrogance:** Under stress, some become abrasive. Others become arrogant because of their brilliance and began to try to intimidate others. Reactions might be "He made others feel stupid."

- **Betrayal of trust:** Dishonesty, one-upmanship, or failure to follow through.

- **Excessive ambition:** Tendency to think only of the next job or playing politics.

- **Specific performance problems with responsibilities:** Failure to meet goals, laziness, or lack of ability to handle new ventures or jobs that needed powers of persuasion. Failure to acknowledge problems, covering them up, or trying to blame them on others.

- **Overmanagement; inability to delegate or to build teams:** After a certain point, a leader must become a manager, someone who sees that the work is done. Inability to make this transition.

- **Inability to staff effectively:** Not able to bring together the right kinds of skills and personalities.

- **Inability to think strategically:** Being caught in a one-way solution approach.

It is very important for a fundraising professional to realize that strengths may become weaknesses. Ambition can be viewed as politicking. Deficiencies eventually matter. Success goes to some managers' heads. After years of being told how good they are, some lose humility and become cold and arrogant. Then information sources begin to dry up because people no longer want to work with them. Events conspire. Sometimes it's just plain "unluck." As an anonymous sage put it, "Careers last a long time. Leave a trail of mistakes and you eventually find yourself encircled by your past."

Perhaps Max De Pree said it best—"Human potential remains a mystery, expressed in more ways than you or I could list. We also know that human potential is often stifled—a great and common tragedy. Perhaps one way to say it is that human potential is best expressed through love—whether love of people, one's God, or one's work. Because most people who work in the nonprofit world would work there for love, maybe we should not be surprised that many nonprofit groups have become places of realized potential."[11]

REFLECTIONS

A philosopher once said that a great fear people have is that of total insignificance. How afraid are you of insignificance? Of failure? How do you describe failure?

Can you identify in yourself any of the following problems that can occur when developing the "new" leader in you? If so, what can you do about these?

- Replicating the poor leadership habits of others in the fundraising profession.

- Lacking basic skills in leadership that makes you more successful in leading up for fundraising success.

- Lacking good models or mentors in the profession.

- Not having formal fundraising training, in the past or currently available.

- Confusion over desirable leadership traits for fundraising and what they mean to you.[12]

---

[11] Max De Pree, *Leading Without Power: Finding Hope in Serving Community* (Holland, MI: Shepherd Foundation, 1997), p. 20.

[12] Adapted from Richard L. Daft and Robert H. Lengel. *Fusion Leadership: Unlocking the Subtle Forces That Change People and Organizations* (San Francisco: Berrett-Koehler, 2000), p. 17.

DEVELOP YOUR SKILLS

Rate yourself on these fatal flaws that may seal the fate of an executive. Ratings are 1–5. Number 1 indicates no problem with the trait, number 5 means you have some changes to make.

Fatal Flaw	Personal Rating	Suggestions for Change and Improvement
Insensitivity to others	1 2 3 4 5	
Coldness, aloofness, arrogance	1 2 3 4 5	
Betrayal of trust	1 2 3 4 5	
Excessive ambition	1 2 3 4 5	
Specific performance problems	1 2 3 4 5	
Over management, inability to delegate or develop teams	1 2 3 4 5	
Inability to staff effectively	1 2 3 4 5	
Inability to think strategically	1 2 3 4 5	

FOR FURTHER READING

Additional readings can be found at the end of the book.

Richard L. Daft and Robert H. Lengel. *Fusion Leadership: Unlocking the Subtle Forces that Change People and Organizations.* San Francisco: Berrett-Koehler, 2000.

Nancy R. Daly. "Characteristics That Count: Nine Leadership Traits That Translate to On-target Actions," *Association Management* (January 2003), pp. 49–52.

Max De Pree. *Leading Without Power: Finding Hope in Serving Community.* Holland, MI: Shepherd Foundation, 1997.

Hans Finzel. *The Top Ten Mistakes Leaders Make.* Colorado Springs: Cook Communications, 2000.

Frances Hesselbein, Marshall Goldsmith, Richard Beckhard, ed. *The Leader of the Future.* New York: The Drucker Foundation, 1996.

CHAPTER 10

Speeding Your Growth in Leadership— Meeting the Challenges

This chapter outlines specific steps to take in order to become an effective leader from any position or rank.

ormer President Gerald Ford was known for his optimism. Part of that optimism shows in his firm belief that leaders are ordinary people with strengths that need to be exercised. He has said that if the proper groundwork can be laid, extraordinary results can be achieved. A good leader believes in long-range benefits, not short-term solutions, and every person with a will to lead can develop those skills.

"Every few years the archaeologists unearth another ancient civilization that flourished for a time and then died. The modern mind, acutely conscious of the sweep of history and chronically apprehensive, is quick to ask, "Is it our turn now?"[1] This statement by John Gardner illustrates the need for renewal by a society and that there is no need or

---

[1] John W. Gardner, *Self-Renewal: The Individual and the Innovative Society* (New York: W. W. Norton, 1981), p. 1.

place for complacency. In the same way, a professional should understand that there is a time for renewal, for exerting effort in making appropriate changes as they are needed and desired. "Renewal is not just innovation and change. It is also the process of bringing the results of change into line with our purposes."[2]

Why do fundraising professionals sometimes drag their feet when it comes to developing leadership qualities? A possible evaluation of this situation is illustrated in the table below.

Sad Facts	Sorry Results and Possible Solutions
"I don't have time!"	When WILL you have time? Will opportunities pass you by? Will job offers quit coming if you're not moving ahead in performance?
"I don't believe in leading from the middle, or leading up!"	You're bucking the tide. Noted experts, researchers, time-honored authors, and other credible individuals all believe leadership takes place in many positions, ranks, responsibilities. It doesn't just come from the top.
"It's going to take too much time; I'm too busy."	Yes, it will take time to practice renewal. It begins with self-awareness, moves to evaluation, and has to involve planning of self-development, and finally the practice of leadership becomes who we are.
"My colleagues are going to think I'm wasting time."	Maybe this is a time to begin practicing leading from the middle. Be an example. Build a study time. Take small steps to show others how you work better (and maybe are a nicer person to work with).
"It's all too confusing."	We've provided options and ideas. Other books abound. Start small. As the old cliché goes, you can't eat a whole elephant all at one time, but you can eat it one bite at a time. Pick one habit to perfect or to discard. Pick one trait to develop. Get a coach. Draw up a plan.
"I don't know where to start!"	That's why this chapter was written!

---

[2] *Ibid.*, p. 6.

Shakespeare spoke of the seven ages of man. Adopting this sage's model, Warren Bennis believes that a leader's life has seven ages as well. He paraphrases Shakespeare's version in *As You Like It* and describes the stages as infant, schoolboy, lover, soldier, general, statesman, and sage.[3] Entertaining as this is, there is some truth to understanding, planning and implementing a workable and personalized approach to learning in stages.

A man—a true believer—on his knees in despair is begging God. "God," he says, "my sweetie, my darling, she needs medicine and I do not have the money. Please, God, please, let me win the lottery."

The next week, he is back on his knees. "God, my God, the loan has come due, I don't have the money. Please, I am begging on my knees, please let me win the lottery."

The man prays and prays to no avail. He becomes more and more frustrated and angry with God for not answering his prayers. Again, a week later, he is back at it." God, please listen to me. I'm desperate, please; please let me win the. . . ."

He is interrupted by an impatient voice booming from above: "Son, help me out—buy a ticket."

Lesson to be applied: Fundraisers can't just wait and let leadership develop; they must have a plan and invest in its development.

—Scott Blanchard and Madeleine Homan[4]

---

[3] Warren G. Bennis, "The Seven Ages of the Leader," *Harvard Business Review* (January 2004), pp. 46–53.

[4] From Scott Blanchard and Madeleine Homan, *Leverage Your Best, Ditch the Rest* (New York: HarperCollins, 2004), p. 27.

Before looking at how you might plan to develop your leadership skills in your profession of fundraising, a perusal of a hierarchy of capabilities explained by Jim Collins in the *Harvard Business Review* is worthwhile. He discusses Level 5 leaders and how necessary they are to organizational change and good leadership.[5] Before looking at level five, however, let's study how one gets to level five.

According to Collins, at Level 1 is the highly capable individual who makes productive contributions through talent, knowledge, skills, and good work habits. At Level 2 is the contributing team member, who adds to the achievement of group objectives and works effectively with others in the group. Level 3 encompasses the competent manager, who organizes people and resources toward the effective and efficient pursuit of predetermined objectives. At Level 4 is the effective leader, who catalyzes commitment to and vigorous pursuit of a clear and compelling vision and stimulates the group to high performance standards. Finally, at Level 5 is the executive who builds enduring greatness through a paradoxical combination of personal humility and professional will.[6] As Collins says, Level 5 leadership is essential for taking an organization from good to great, but it's not the only factor. It enables implementation of other findings. Many of these apply well to the fundraising professional.

First, good-to-great leaders attend to people first and strategy second. They maintain the belief that they can surmount obstacles and prevail at the end. Level 5 leaders understand that transformations do not happen overnight but in incremental steps. And, Level 5 leaders are disciplined in thought and action. His conclusions? "There are two categories of people: Those who don't have the Level 5 seed within

---

[5] Jim Collins, "Level 5 Leadership: The Triumph of Humility and Fierce Resolve," *Harvard Business Review* (January 2001).

[6] *Ibid.,* p. 70.

them and those who do!"[7] Those who do have Level 5 possibilities may, under the right circumstances such as self-reflection, acquiring a mentor, or having a significant life experience, begin to develop a Level 5 capacity. Not all who are Level 5 leaders are top executives. What is at the heart of this theory is that Level 5 characteristics, moving from good to great, can be found in most of us.

So, we need to develop our plan to move ahead, from good to great. Deepak Sethi, who is a past director of executive and leadership development for the Thomson Corporation, identified six critical skills to lead effectively from the middle. The development of these skills should not only serve as our foundation for planning but also guide us in establishing the content of the plan.

1. **Self-Awareness:** Avoid blind spots, tap into trusted sources of feedback, and act upon honest feedback.

2. **Bird's-Eye Perspective:** Don't lose sight of the big picture. Don't limit your ability to transfer or create new knowledge.

3. **Emotional Competence:** Don't get derailed because of a lack of empathy and fundamental people skills.

4. **Advanced Communication Skills:** Use effective persuasion and presentation of ideas.

5. **Career Management Skills:** Network both inside and outside of the organization as you hone your skills.

6. **Continuous Learning:** When we change, our world changes. Know how to learn and seek opportunities for learning.[8]

---

[7] *Ibid.*, p. 74.

[8] Deepak Sethi, "Leading From the Middle," *Leader to Leader* (Summer 2000).

Donna Shalala, former secretary of the Department of Health and Human Services; chancellor of the University of Wisconsin, Madison; current president of the University of Miami; board member; and scholar says, "Being a good leader requires the ability to work with all kinds of people and to listen to them. When you are the head of an agency, you're a member of a team. You are always a member of a team, whether you're part of a cabinet or whether it's a team you put together."[9]

Nancy Daly, writing in the journal *Association Management,* listed nine traits that lead to effective leadership. These also can provide us with reminders of what we must attain as characteristics if we are going to practice more leading up! The first is trust. Leaders earn trust through their behavior. They act with integrity and are honest and respectful. This leads to the second trait, which is respect. This is a two-way street because a leader is respected for his or her expertise, but effective leaders respect others as well. Third is vision, the ability to see the big picture and how the mission interacts with external and internal forces. Fourth is self-confidence, having a presence that indicates we know our strengths and weakness, and in spite of the latter, we are self-assured. Communication skills, the fifth trait, can make or break the leader's ability achieve results. Being articulate in expressing the mission, the need, and the difference a donor can make leads to much success in fundraising. Enthusiasm is sixth; passion is contagious because an enthusiastic leader can mobilize staff, leaders, volunteers, and donors. Giving feedback is number seven—the ability to praise and recognize, as well as give instructive and productive input. The ability to fulfill

---

[9] Quoted in Jane Eisinger, "Secrets of Her Success," *Association Management* (January 2002), p. 73.

commitments certainly lies at the heart of successful fundraising practice. And finally, growing more leaders—sharing our abilities and our knowledge to perpetuate excellence in leadership for fundraising.[10]

As we put together the picture of an effective leader who can and does lead up in the fundraising profession, who effectively provides leadership from any position or rank, let's turn to a model presented in *Profiles of Excellence,* a study of effective leaders and leadership. This adaptation of their characteristics and questions for self-analysis can, perhaps, provide you with a start toward a plan for developing skills in leading up.[11]

1. **A guiding vision:** What is your long-range vision for your organization and are you satisfied with it? What process are you following in developing this vision? How would you modify your vision as you begin to exert more leadership from your present position? Have you challenged the status quo?

2. **Conveying the vision to others:** How do you communicate your expectations for the organization to others? What have been your greatest challenges in gaining acceptance of your vision and getting people excited by it? What has been your success in attracting and energizing volunteers and donors? What approaches do you find most effective?

3. **Knowing oneself:** What new things have you learned about yourself in the past year and how did you learn them. What changes in your behavior or attitude would you like to make and

---

[10] Nancy R. Daly, "Characteristics That Count: Nine Leadership Traits That Translate to On-target Actions," *Association Management* (January 2003), pp. 49–52.

[11] E. G. Knauft, Renee A. Berger, and Sandra T. Gray, *Profiles of Excellence: Achieving Success in the Nonprofit Sector* (San Francisco: Jossey-Bass, 1991).

how will you accomplish these? How often do you take stock of yourself? What is the outcome?

4. **Standing by your convictions:** How would people who know you describe your ability to take a stand on a controversial issue? What is reasonable compromise for you? What tough decisions have you made about your work as a fundraiser? What were the outcomes and what did you think of them?

5. **Taking risks:** Can you cite some risks you have taken, including examples where the outcome was uncertain, the funding was unsure, and the board and staff harbored doubts? What was involved in reaching the decision? What mistakes have you made as a result of your decisions? How did you react to these and what did you learn from them? What would motivate you to make a decision that has a 50 percent chance of failing?

6. **Mastering the organization:** What are examples of how you have changed your organization to help it better achieve its mission and adapt to your vision of its potential? How do you differentiate between change for its own sake and a constructive change in the status quo? Once changes are made, how do you maintain the enthusiasm and excellence you have achieved?[12]

When you develop a leadership style that's right for you, your work as a fundraiser, and your organization, you will enjoy higher productivity

---

[12] Adapted from E. G. Knauft, Renee A. Berger, and Sandra T. Gray, *Profiles of Excellence: Achieving Success in the Nonprofit Sector* (San Francisco: Jossey-Bass, 1991).

and increased morale, plus the satisfaction of having achieved your goals for leading up!

REFLECTIONS

Suppose that you were to develop a "backward plan." This type of planning has become increasingly popular because it is perhaps more realistic than some traditional plans. First you identify the outcome you wish to achieve. In the case of this chapter, think about how you want to be perceived as a leader in your role as a fundraising professional. Then, work backward, identifying the steps you will need to take in order to get there. Organize and reorganize these steps so that there is logical flow between each one until you reach your outcome. In *How to Think Like Leonardo da Vinci* by Michael J. Gelb, a section titled "Fix Your Course to a Star" explains, "The most carefully crafted strategies rarely work out exactly according to plan. But the best improvisers do not just 'wing it,' they start with a well-made plan and then adapt gracefully to changing circumstances. You are the captain of your own ship, but you can't control the weather. Sometimes life brings us smooth sailing; other times we get squalls, hurricanes, and tsunamis. Leonardo counseled, 'He who fixes his course to a star changes not.' Fix your course to a star, and be ready to navigate through storms and uncharted icebergs."[13]

So, engage in some reflective planning. Use the format illustrated in Exhibit 10.1, if it works for you.

---

[13] Michael J. Gelb, *How to Think Like Leonardo da Vinci* (New York: Dell, 1998), p. 256.

EXHIBIT 10.1   REFLECTIVE PLANNING

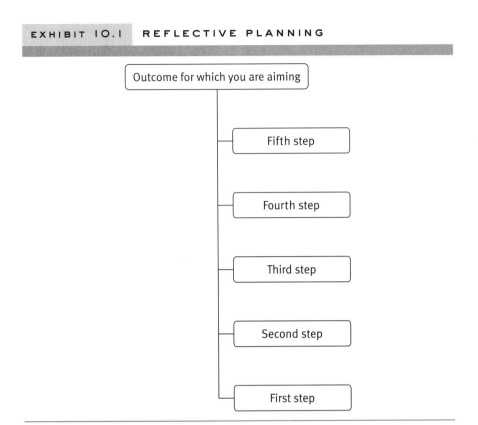

DEVELOP YOUR SKILLS

Polishing Gifts (adapted from Max DePree).[14] Opportunities for developing one's leadership abilities abound. We need to think of long-term potential and opportunity. Leaders polish all their facets equally. Professional and career development is not enough. Leaders see a twofold opportunity—to build a life and to build a career. Polishing gifts requires us to think broadly and deeply, to understand what we believe, and to be directed internally as well as externally.

---

[14] Max De Pree, *Leadership Jazz* (New York: Dell 1992), chapter on polishing gifts, pp. 166–184.

Question to Consider	Your Answer and/or Action Step
How do I learn best? Reading, listening, conversation, technology?	
What settings or groups lead to my most productive times?	
How do I feel about working with a mentor? What kind of mentor? How would I do this?	
Am I willing to reserve time for reflection?	
What do I need in order to cultivate my potential? Schooling, opportunities, people?	
How will I nourish the spiritual, the visionary, the qualitative side of my life?	
What kind of legacy do I want to leave?	
What satisfies my entire existence— the tangible or the intangible? What would I list under my choice?	
What kind of power is important to me? How do I develop such power?	
What REALLY gives meaning to my life? Is my life in balance? If not, what parts are not and how will I work on balancing these?	

FOR FURTHER READING

Additional readings can be found at the end of the book.

Warren G. Bennis and Robert J. Thomas. *Geeks and Geezers: How Era, Values and Defining Moments Shape Leaders* (Boston: Harvard Business School Press, 2002).

Jim Collins. "Level 5 Leadership: The Triumph of Humility and Fierce Resolve," *Harvard Business Review* (January 2001).

Nancy R. Daly. "Characteristics That Count: Nine Leadership Traits That Translate to On-target Actions," *Association Management* (January 2003), pp. 49–52.

Frances Hesselbein, editor-in-chief. *Leader to Leader,* San Francisco: Peter F. Drucker Foundation for Nonprofit Management and Jossey-Bass.

Deepak Sethi. "Leading From the Middle," *Leader to Leader* (Summer 2000).

CHAPTER 11

Take Me to Your Leader!
Leadership That Gets Results

Conclusions, a review of concepts, inspirational and
motivational advice, reaffirmation of the concept of leading
from the middle, and a look at "what happens now."

The photograph is of no commercial value." So said Thomas Edison, remarking on his own invention in 1880. "There is no likelihood man can ever tap the power of the atom." This was statement was made by Robert Millikan, a Nobel prize winner in physics, in 1920. The American Road Congress said in 1913, "It is an idle dream to imagine that automobiles will take the place of railways in the long-distance movement of passengers." And, given that this book was, of course, written on a computer, "I think there is a world market for about five computers," was stated in 1943 by Thomas Watson, chairman of IBM, and "There is no reason for any individual to have a computer in their home," was a comment by Ken Olsen, president of Digital Equipment Corporation, 1977.[1]

---

[1] Quoted in many sources, but taken from Hans Finzel, *The Top Ten Mistakes Leaders Make* (Colorado Springs, CO: Cook Communications, 2000), p. 73.

What can we predict for the future of leadership in the fundraising profession, where every person can be and is a leader? Now that the groundwork and the plans have been laid, what remains to be suggested? As Clark Aldrich put it in "The New Core of Leadership," "Getting two advocates to agree on a definition of *leadership* seems impossible. Covey, Blanchard, PDI, DDI, Kotter, and AchieveGlobal (just to name a few) compete tooth and nail. Many consultants have tried (and failed) to turn leadership into a cookbook-style skill, handing out recipes for anyone to follow. Meanwhile, thousands of academics have heaped up layers of philosophical debate that make leadership undefinable, almost magical. . . . Now, it seems, everything good is due to leadership and everything bad is due to lack of leadership."[2]

The director of an orchestra may perhaps serve as a useful model for some of the important relationships which run through all leadership situations.

Players must have training for their roles. Not all group failures are the boss's fault. Toscanini could not get great music from a high school band.

A conductor must set up his ground rules, his signals, and his tastes in such a way that the mechanics of getting a rehearsal started do not interfere with the musical purpose.

The musicians must share satisfaction with their leader in the production of music or of music of a certain quality. Unless they individually achieve a sense of accomplishment or even fulfillment, his leadership has failed and he will not make great music.[3]

—W.C.H. Prentice[3]

---

[2] Clark Aldrich, "The New Core of Leadership," *Training and Development* (April 2003), p. 34.

[3] Quoted and adapted from W.C.H. Prentice, "Understanding Leadership," *Harvard Business Review* (January 2004).

After this mild diatribe, Aldrich does say, "But, in fact, the leadership planets may finally be aligning. Across the wealth of content out there, a common consensus about leadership is emerging. Experts may disagree on the fringes, but they're remarkably aligned on the core. Like quality, leadership is usable, diagnosable, and, yes, teachable."[4]

That's what we're trying to accomplish—to help ourselves, as fundraising professionals, see that leadership is teachable and, furthermore, "learnable." Fortunately, as the venerable Peter Koestenbaum stated, the leadership mind is spacious and can handle the ambiguities of this world, conflicting feelings and contradictory ideas.[5] He said that progress in leadership development requires commitment to two things. "First, you need to dedicate yourself to understanding yourself better—in the philosophical sense of understanding what it means to exist as a human being in the world. Second, you need to change your habits of thought: how you think, what you value, how you work, how you connect with people, how you learn, what you expect from life, and how you manage frustration. Changing those habits means changing your way of being intelligent. It means moving from a nonleadership mind to a leadership mind."[6]

In the Epilogue of *Leading Without Power: Finding Hope in Serving Community,* Max De Pree describes the seemingly hopeless summer of 1941, as the German army approached Leningrad. The staff of the Hermitage Museum packed up tens of thousands of paintings and sculptures, antiquities, and treasures, to be shipped east, away from the Germans and the upcoming siege. The staff left the empty frames and pedestals in their proper places in the museum as a sign of their conviction that someday they would be able to restore the Hermitage and

---

[4] Aldrich, "The New Core of Leadership," p. 34.

[5] Polly Labarre. "Do You Have the Will to Lead?" *Fast Company* (March 2000).

[6] Labarre, "Do You Have the Will to Lead?" p. 224.

its priceless collection of art. Though they were losing their art, they were determined not to lose hope.

The German armies surrounded Leningrad for more than two years, and the Russians endured that long and arduous time with little to eat and often under attack. The staff of the Hermitage and their families moved to the basement of the building, determined to save it. Russian soldiers and citizens came regularly to help clean up the damage done by the artillery. As a way of saying thank you, the staff conducted tours of the museum for these people. Of course the art wasn't there. Pictures show the Hermitage curators conducting tours, with soldiers and citizens standing in front of empty picture frames and forlorn pedestals. The curators described from memory and in great detail the art, filling in the blank spaces in the wonderful museum with their own dedication, commitment, and love.

This exemplifies vision, service, commitment, and leadership. This is what it means to see what others may not see and move to the potential

> *Leadership requires timing, intuition, and personalization. It's about the when and the how, not just the what. It's about leveraging relationships, not rules. It's a much more critical skill than quality. The payoff in all environments to bring together rigor and control with creativity and empowerment can transform lives, enterprises, and industries. We have the opportunity to foster and instill a new genre of leadership as part of our personas and corporate cultures. To bring it into our organizations, we now have to role model, not just mandate, leadership.*
>
> —Clark Aldrich[7]

---

[7] Clark Aldrich, "The New Core of Leadership," *Training and Development* (April 2003), p. 37.

of the organization's and individual's fulfillment. This, then, is providing leadership without having recognizable and identifiable power and status.

As Peter Koestenbaum said, "Some people are more talented than others. Some are more educationally privileged than others. But we all have the capacity to be great. Greatness comes with recognizing that your potential is limited only by how you choose, how you use your freedom, how resolute you are, how persistent you are—in short, by your attitude. And we are all free to choose our attitude."[8]

REFLECTIONS

Analyze yourself; determine what three things you wish to accomplish when leading up; make a "backwards plan" for just these three things; discuss your plan with a trusted mentor, colleague or friend; revise your plan; then go out, celebrate, eat some chocolate, and reflect. Now you're on your way to becoming an effective leader, one who can lead up, because it all starts with self-awareness, moves to self-regulation and action, and ends with the adoption of the leadership trait you are striving to acquire.

_____

_____

_____

_____

_____

_____

_____

---

[8] Labarre, "Do You Have the Will to Lead?" p. 230.

DEVELOP YOUR SKILLS

Mahatma Gandhi said, "You must be the change you wish to see in the world." Here are some tips for self-leadership. In the second column, write down what suggestions you have for yourself and perhaps for others. Some suggestions are given on subsequent pages. You might want to fill in your own "clues" (that is, suggestions) first, and then see what the suggestions given here are.[9]

Leadership Quality	Clues for Accomplishing the Quality
The quality of our leadership is reflected in our relationships with donors, colleagues, supervisors, and others in our work world.	
Renewing ourselves as leaders requires continuous learning.	
We must recognize and evaluate our leadership talents so that we can benefit from the past as we look ahead to the present.	
Actual changes occur best if our mental images are clear.	

(continues)

---

[9] The idea for this form came from Frances Hesselbein, Marshall Goldsmith, Richard Beckhard, eds., *The Leader of the Future* (New York: The Drucker Foundation, 1996), and was revised and adapted with a focus on fundrasing and leading up.

Leadership Quality	Clues for Accomplishing the Quality
Assessment of our leadership qualities is best done from our own perspective rather than from someone else's incomplete evaluation of who we are.	
We can choose the criteria to which we want our leadership to measure up.	
We need not be victims to external forces. We can control our time and our efforts.	
A clear sense of personal purpose helps us reach fulfillment and aids in avoiding anxiety in times of stress.	
The key to high performance is integrity—doing what we have promised.	
Success and celebration attract others.	
We must be accountable to our publics if we are to gain respect.	

Leadership Quality	Suggested Clues for Accomplishment
The quality of our leadership is reflected in our relationships with donors, colleagues, supervisors, and others in our work world.	*We should consciously be responsive to those who depend on us, from our donors to our employees. Sometimes this is expressed in simple ways, like how quickly we answer communication that comes to us, or how we express appreciation.*
Renewing ourselves as leaders requires continuous learning.	*We should challenge ourselves to move out of the comfort zone. We should also take time to reflect on what we're doing we're doing and how we're doing it. New learning experiences can be part of our professional planning and development.*
We must recognize and evaluate our leadership talents so that we can benefit from the past as we look ahead to the present.	*If we love what we're doing we can overlook, up to a point, lack of time, tiredness, or even discouragement. If our work is "just a job," it's much more difficult to remain enthusiastic. Part of our responsibility is to recognize our own talents and be justifiably proud of them. We should avoid thinking "everyone else does better than I do," because such thoughts are self-defeating.*
Actual changes occur best if our mental images are clear.	*If we picture ourselves doing exceptional work, we are much more likely to actually do so. Having a clear mental image of what we will and can do helps in the accomplishment of those goals.*
Assessment of our leadership qualities is best done from our own perspective rather than from someone else's incomplete evaluation of who we are.	*If we're honest with ourselves, we can evaluate our strengths and weaknesses the best. At we do this, then it's good to get another perspective and see how they match.*

(continues)

Leadership Quality	Suggested Clues for Accomplishment
We can choose the criteria to which we want our leadership to measure up.	There are many leadership theories and best practices. There are many authors and researchers who have put these in writing. We can choose those which we believe we can best adopt and adapt, and which will best serve us for carrying out our personal and organizational goals.
We need not be victims to external forces. We can control our time and our efforts.	There may be times when bad situations are out of our control, or when we truly can't find better jobs or can't change our circumstances, but most of the time we CAN take control. It's up to us to make our best choices and change those choices if we made mistakes.
A clear sense of personal purpose helps us reach fulfillment and aids in avoiding anxiety in times of stress.	If we know where we're headed, we will have the joy of accomplishment. If we have a clear purpose, then whatever tough times come, we will forge ahead because we know where we're headed.
The key to high performance is integrity—doing what we have promised.	Gaining others' trust is vital in motivating others to take action toward goals. Besides, ethical practice is our obligation when we have the trust of our donors and our organizations to consider.
Success and celebration attract others.	When we and our organizations have achieved notable goals, we should share the credit and give appropriate recognition to those who helped us get there. Everyone loves a winner and enjoys a celebration that says we're the winners!
We must be accountable to our publics if we are to gain respect.	Openness in what we do, showing evidence of good stewardship, is critical for gaining and achieving respect.

Recommended Readings

Karl Albrecht. *The Northbound Train*. New York: AMACOM, 1994.

Clark Aldrich. "Using Leadership to Implement Leadership," *Training and Development* (May 2003), pp. 95–114.

Clark Aldrich. "The New Core of Leadership," *Training and Development* (April 2003), pp. 32–37.

Haidee Allerton. "Leadership A to Z: An Interview with James O'Toole," *Training and Development* (March 2000).

Stephen Ambrose, Ph.D. "Inspiration: From Meriwether Lewis of Lewis & Clark Fame," *Bottom Line Personal* (September 1, 1996).

Dean Anderson and Linda S. Ackerman Anderson. *Beyond Change Management: Advanced Strategies for Today's Transformational Leaders*. San Francisco: Jossey-Bass/Pfeiffer, 2001.

Helen Astin and Carole Leland. *Women of Influence, Women of Vision: A Cross-Generational Study of Leaders and Social Change*. San Francisco: Jossey-Bass, 1991.

Alan Axelrod. *Elizabeth I, CEO: Strategic Lessons from the Leader Who Built an Empire*. Paramus, NJ: Prentice Hall, 2000.

Joseph L. Badaracco, Jr. *Leading Quietly*. Boston: Harvard Business School Press, 2002.

Joseph L. Badaracco, Jr. "We Don't Need Another Hero," *Harvard Business Review* (September 2001).

Robert Barner. "Five Steps to Leadership Competencies," *Training and Development* (March 2000).

Bernard M. Bass. *Stogdill's Handbook of Leadership.* New York: The Free Press, a Division of Macmillan, third edition, 1990.

Bernard M. Bass. "Stogdill's Handbook of Leadership: What are the Qualities That Mark the Effective Leader?" *Soundview Executive Book Summaries,* (March 1986) volume 8, number 3, part 2.

Geoffrey M. Bellman. *Getting Things Done When You Are Not in Charge: How to Succeed from a Support Position.* San Francisco: Berrett-Koehler, 1992.

William J. Bennett. *Virtues of Leadership* Nashville, TN: W Publishing Co., a division of Thomas Nelson, 2001.

Warren G. Bennis. "The Seven Ages of the Leader," *Harvard Business Review* (January 2004), pp. 46–53.

Warren Bennis and Robert J. Thomas. *Geeks and Geezers: How Era, Values and Defining Moments Shape Leaders.* Boston: Harvard Business School Press, pp. 2–3.

Warren Bennis. *On Becoming a Leader.* Reading, MA: Addison-Wesley, 1994.

Warren Bennis. "Lessons in Leadership from Superconsultant Warren Bennis," *Bottom Line Personal* (July 1, 1996).

Sheila Murray Bethel. "The Twelve Qualities of Leadership," *Career Guild,* volume 9, number 2 (second quarter 1986).

Sheila Murray Bethel. *Beyond Management to Leadership: Designing the 21st Century Association.* Washington, DC: The Foundation of the American Society of Association Executives, 1993.

Ed Betof. "Leaders as Teachers," *Training and Development,* volume 58, number 3 (March 2004), pp. 55–63.

Elaine Biech, ed. *The Pfeiffer Book of Successful Team-Building Tools.* San Francisco: Jossey-Bass/Pfeiffer, 2001.

Stanley Bing. *Throwing the Elephant: Zen and the Art of Managing Up.* New York: HarperCollins, 2002.

Scott Blanchard and Madeleine Homan. *Leverage Your Best, Ditch the Rest.* New York: HarperCollins, 2004.

Don Blohowiak. "Real Leaders for Unreal Times," *Association Management* (January 2002), pp. 42–48.

Lee G. Bolman and Terrence E. Deal. "Leadership and the Meaning of Life," *MLE Alumni Bulletin,* vol. 8, no. 2 (June 1995).

Lee G. Bolman and Terrence E. Deal. *Leading with Soul: An Uncommon Journey of Spirit.* San Francisco: Jossey-Bass, 2001.

Deborah Brody. "First Among Equals," *Foundation News* (September–October 1992).

R. Scott Brunner, CAE. "When Realtors Read Plato," *Association Management* (February 1999).

William C. Byham. "How to Create a Reservoir of Ready-Made Leaders," *Training and Development* (March 2000).

Erik Calonius. "Take Me to Your Leader," *Hemispheres* (April 1995).

David D. Chrislip and Carl E. Larson. *Skills for a New Kind of Leadership: Collaborative Leadership—How Citizens and Civic Leaders Make a Difference.* San Francisco: Jossey Bass, 1994.

David D. Chrislip and Carl E. Larson. "Skills for a New Kind of Leadership," *Leadership IS* (March 1995).

Kenneth E. Clark and Miriam B. Clark. "Definitions and Dimensions of Leadership," *Leadership IS,* 1994.

M. Carolyn Clark, Rosemary S. Caffarella, and Peggy B. Ingram. "Women in Leadership: Living with Constraints of the Glass Ceiling," *Initiatives,* volume 59, number 1.

Jim Collins. "Level 5 Leadership: The Triumph of Humility and Fierce Resolve," *Harvard Business Review,* January 2001.

Jay A. Conger. *Learning to Lead: The Art of Transforming Managers into Leaders.* San Francisco: Jossey-Bass, 1992.

Richard M. Cyert. "Defining Leadership and Explicating the Process," *Nonprofit Management & Leadership,* volume 1, number 1 (Fall 1990).

Richard L. Daft and Robert H. Lengel. *Fusion Leadership: Unlocking the Subtle Forces that Change People and Organizations.* San Francisco: Berrett-Koehler, 2000.

Nancy R. Daly. "Characteristics That Count: Nine Leadership Traits That Translate to On-target Actions," *Association Management* (January 2003), pp. 49–52.

Max De Pree. *Leadership Jazz.* New York: Dell 1992.

Max De Pree. *Leading Without Power: Finding Hope in Serving Community.* Holland, MI: Shepherd Foundation, 1997.

Peter F. Drucker. *The Effective Executive.* New York: HarperCollins, 1993.

Jane Eisinger. "A Man with a Mission," *Association Management* (February 2001).

Jane Eisinger. "Window to the World," *Association Management* (October 2001).

Jane Eisinger. "Secrets of Her Success," *Association Management* (January 2002), pp. 72–74.

Dayton Fandray. "Lombardi's Lessons," *Continental* (January 2004), pp. 27–28.

Hans Finzel. *The Top Ten Mistakes Leaders Make.* Colorado Springs: Cook Communications, 2000.

Roger Fisher and Alan Sharp. *Getting it Done: How to Lead When You're Not in Charge.* New York: Harper Business, 1998.

John W. Gardner. "Exploring Leadership," *Leadership News* (Fall 1984).

John W. Gardner. "The Nature of Leadership: Introductory Considerations," *Independent Sector* (January 1986).

John W. Gardner. *Self-Renewal: The Individual and the Innovative Society.* New York: W. W. Norton, 1981.

John W. Gardner. *On Leadership.* New York: The Free Press, a Division of Macmillan, 1990.

John W. Gardner. "Remarks by John W. Gardner," *Leadership USA* (November 19, 1995).

G. Worth George. "Leadership Jazz: Selected Themes for Orchestrating Nonprofit Quality," *Nonprofit World,* volume 2, No. 2 (March–April 1993).

Seth Godin. "Survival Enough," *Fast Company* (January 2002).

Daniel Goleman. "Leadership That Gets Results," *Harvard Business Review* (March–April 2000), accessed at Harvard Business Online, Product #4487.

Daniel Goleman. "What Makes a Leader?" *Harvard Business Review* (January 2004), pp. 82–91.

John H. Graham IV. "The Mark of a Leader," *Association Management* (January 2004), p. 16.

Sandra T. Gray, CAE. "Fostering Leadership for the New Millennium," *Leadership,* 1995.

Robert K. Greenleaf. *Servant: Retrospect and Prospect.* Indianapolis: The Robert K. Greenleaf Center, 1990.

Robert K. Greenleaf. *Servant Leadership: A Journey into the Nature of Legitimate Power and Greatness.* New York: Paulist Press, 1977.

Gene Griessman. *The Words Lincoln Lived By.* New York: Fireside/Simon & Schuster, 1997.

Harvard Business Review on Leadership. Boston: Harvard Business School Publishing, 1998.

Howard Haas and Bob Tamarkin. *The Leader Within: An Empowering Path of Self-Discovery.* New York: Harper Business, 1992.

Steven F. Hayward. *Churchill on Leadership: Executive Success in the Face of Adversity.* Rocklin, CA Forum, 1998.

John Heider. *The Tao of Leadership: Lao Tzu's Tao Te Ching Adapted for a New Age.* New York: Bantam Books, 1986.

Ronald Heifetz. *Leadership Without Easy Answers.* Cambridge: Belknap Press of Harvard University, 1994.

Cynthia M. Hernandez and Donald R. Leslie. "Charismatic Leadership: The Aftermath," *Nonprofit Management & Leadership,* volume 11, number 4 (Summer 2001).

Frances Hesselbein, Marshall Goldsmith, and Richard Beckhard, eds. *The Leader of the Future.* New York: The Drucker Foundation, 1996.

Frances Hesselbein, editor-in-chief. *Leader to Leader.* San Francisco: Peter F. Drucker Foundation for Nonprofit Management and Jossey-Bass.

"How to Lead When You're Not the Boss," *Harvard Management Update,* a newsletter from Harvard Business School Publishing, volume 5, number 3 (March 2000).

Elizabeth Jeffries. *The Heart of Leadership: Influencing by Design.* Dubuque, IA: Kendall/Hunt, 1992.

James M. Jenkes. "Speeding Your Growth with Leadership Skills," *Communication Briefings,* volume 9, number 10 (August 1990).

Rosabeth Moss Kanter. "The Middle Manager as Innovator, *Harvard Business Review* (July–August 2004), pp. 150–161.

Barbara Kellerman. "Leadership–6 and All," *Harvard Business Review* (January 2004), pp. 40–45.

Barbara Kellerman and Larraine R. Matusak, eds. *Cutting Edge Leadership 2000.* College Park, MD: University of Maryland, The James Mac-Gregor Burns Academy of Leadership, 2000.

Walter Kiechel, III. "The Leader as Servant," *Fortune* (May 4,1992).

E. G. Knauft, Renee A. Berger, and Sandra T. Gray. *Profiles of Excellence: Achieving Success in the Nonprofit Sector.* San Francisco: Jossey-Bass, 1991.

John P. Kotter. *The Leadership Factor.* New York: Free Press, 1988.

John P. Kotter. *Leading Change.* Boston : Harvard Business School Press, 1996.

John P. Kotter. "What Leaders Really Do," *Harvard Business Review* (December 2001), pp. 85–96.

James M. Kouzes and Barry Z. Posner. *The Leadership Challenge: How to Get Extraordinary Things Done in Organizations.* San Francisco: Jossey-Bass, 1987.

Roderick M. Kramer. "The Harder They Fall," *Harvard Business Review* (October 2003), pp. 58–66.

Polly Labarre. "Do You Have the Will to Lead?" *Fast Company* (March 2000).

Polly Labarre. "Report From the Future: After Shock," *Fast Company,* January 2002.

Eric H. F. Law. *The Wolf Shall Dwell with the Lamb: A Spirituality for Leadership in a Multicultural Community.* St. Louis: Chalice Press, 1993.

William Lawler. "The Consortium Approach to Grooming Future Leaders," *Training and Development* (March 2000).

"Leadership Development," *Infoline,* ASTD (January 2001).

The Leadership Secrets of Santa Claus. Dallas: The Walk the Talk Company, 2003.

"Leading by Feel," *Harvard Business Review,* January 2004, pp. 27–37.

Robert J. Lee, and Sara N. King, and the Center for Creative Leadership. *Discovering the Leader in You: A Guide to Realizing Your Personal Leadership Potential.* San Francisco: Jossey-Bass, 2001.

Carl Levesque. "A Matter of Being" (Interview with Frances Hesselbein), *Association Management* (January 2003), pp. 63–66.

Mary Lippitt. "How to Influence Leaders," *Training and Development* (March 1999).

Richard Lynch. "A Leader's Task: Reinforce the Values that Drive your Organization," *The Nonprofit Board Report* (October 1994).

Richard Lynch. "Designing Empowering Jobs: Are You a Manager or a Leader?" *The Nonprofit Board Report,* volume 3, number 41 (February 1, 1995).

Barbara Mackoff, and Gary Wenet. *The Inner Work of Leaders: Leadership as a Habit of Mind.* New York: AMACOM, 2001.

John C. Maxwell. *The 21 Irrefutable Laws of Leadership.* Nashville, TN: Thomas Nelson, 1998.

John C. Maxwell, *The 21 Indispensable Qualities of a Leader.* Nashville, TN: Thomas Nelson, 1999.

John C. Maxwell. *Failing Forward: Turning Mistakes into Stepping-Stones for Success.* Nashville, TN: Thomas Nelson, 2000.

Lynne Joy McFarland, Larry E. Senn, and John R. Childress. *21st Century Leadership: Dialogues with 100 Top Leaders.* New York: The Leadership Press, 1993.

Pat McLagan. "Claim Your Change Power," *Training and Development* (October 2001).

Mort Meyerson. "Everything I Thought I Knew About Leadership Is Wrong," in John R. Schermerhorn, *Handbook of the Business Revolution*. Hoboken: John Wiley & Sons, 2001.

Jan Morris. *Lincoln: A Foreigner's Quest*. New York: Simon & Schuster, 2000.

Lance Morrow. "The Real Points of Light," *Time* (December 5, 1994).

Burt Nanus and Stephen M. Dobbs. *Leaders Who Make a Difference: Essential Strategies for Meeting the Nonprofit Challenge*. San Francisco: Jossey-Bass, 1999.

Laura Nash, and Howard Stevenson. "Success That Lasts," *Harvard Business Review* (February 2004), pp. 102–109.

Robert P. Neuschel. *The Servant Leader: Unleashing the Power of Your People*. East Lansing, MI: Visions Sports Management Group, 1998.

Lynn R. Offermann. "When Followers Become Toxic," *Harvard Business Review* (January 2004), pp. 54–60.

Randy Pennington and Marc Bockmon. *On My Honor, I Will: Leading with Integrity in Changing Times* (Foreword by Zig Ziglar). Shippensburg, PA: Destiny Image, 1995.

Tom Peters. "Leading in the real and ragged world," *Indianapolis Business Journal* (February 22, 1993).

Tom Peters. "Rule #3: Leadership Is Confusing as Hell," *Fast Company* (March 2001).

Donald T. Phillips. *Lincoln on Leadership*. New York: Warner Books, 1992.

William C. Pollard. "Mission as an Organizing Principle," *Leader to Leader*, no. 16 (Spring 1000).

Jeffrey Preffer. "Six Characteristics of Leaders who Influence Others Effectively," *The Nonprofit Board Report* (May 1993).

Joseph A. Raelin. "The Myth of Charismatic Leaders," *Training and Development* (March 2003), pp. 47–54.

Joseph A. Raelin. "Preparing for Leaderful Practice," *Training and Development,* Alexandria, VA: ASTD, volume 58, number 3 (March 2004), pp. 65–70.

Frederick F. Reichheld. "Lead for Loyalty," *Harvard Business Review,* July–August 2001.

Kellogg Leadership Studies Project, 1994–1997. *Rethinking Leadership.* College Park, MD: The Burns Academy of Leadership Press, 1998.

Wess Roberts. *Leadership Secrets of Attila the Hun.* New York: Warner Books, 1987.

Steven B. Sample. *The Contrarian's Guide to Leadership.* San Francisco: Jossey-Bass, 2002.

Len Schlesinger. "It Doesn't Take a Wizard to Build a Better Boss," in John R. Schermerhorn, *Handbook of the Business Revolution.* Hoboken: John Wiley & Sons, 2001.

John P. Schuster. "Transforming Your Leadership Style," *Leadership,* 1994.

Roger Schwarz. "Becoming a Facilitative Leader," *Training and Development* (April 2003), pp. 51–57.

Clare Segal, and Bernard Ross. "Leadership through Strategic Thinking," *The Management Center,* July 10–13, 2000.

Deepak Sethi. "Leading From the Middle," *Leader to Leader* (Summer 2000).

Robert Slater. *Get Better or Get Beaten! 29 Leadership Secrets from GE's Jack Welch.* New York: McGraw-Hill, 2001.

John P. Schuster. "Transforming your Leadership Style," *Association Management* (January 1994), volume 46, number 1, p. L39.

Larry C. Spears and Michele Lawrence. *Focus on Leadership: Servant-Leadership for the Twenty-First Century.* Hoboken: John Wiley & Sons, 2002.

Robert E. Staub, II. *The Heart of Leadership: 12 Practices of Courageous Leaders.* Provo, UT: Executive Excellence Publishing, 2000.

Craig R. Taylor and Cindy Wheatley-Lovoy, "Leadership: Lessons From the Magic Kingdom," *Training and Development,* July 1998.

The Forbes Leadership Library. Chicago: *Thoughts on Leadership.* Triumph Books, 1995.

Noel M. Tichy, with Eli Cohen. *The Leadership Engine: How Winning Companies Build Leaders at Every Level.* New York: HarperCollins Publishers, 1997.

"The Tides of Talent," *Training and Development* (April 2003), pp. 34–38.

"What Is Our Common Sense of Leadership?" *Firethorn Quarterly,* issue 1 (Spring 1993).

William S. White. *The Challenge of Nonprofit Leadership: Building a Transformed World,* Charles Stewart Mott Foundation (November 2001).

Garry Willis. *Certain Trumpets: The Call of Leaders.* New York: Simon & Schuster, 1994.

Jean Wills. "Pearls from Past Leaders: Using History's Lessons to Guide Leadership Decisions in a Multicultural World, *Association Management* (February 2003), pp. 61–64.

Marie C. Wilson. *Closing the Leadership Gap.* New York: Penguin Group, 2004.

Steve Yearout, Gerry Miles, and Richard Koonce. "Wanted: Leader-Builders," *Training and Development* (March 2000).

Jack Zenger, Dave Ulrich, and Norm Smallwood. "The New Leadership Development," *Training and Development* (March 2000).

Index